# LEAD
# TO
# LIFT
# UP
# OTHERS

---

Leadership Insights From
A Caregiver's Journey

Ross P.
Woodstock

Edited by Amy Bell, WritePunch Inc.

Designed by www.bookclaw.com

ISBN 978-0-578-77624-8

# PRAISE FOR
## Lead to Lift Up Others

*"Ross takes you on his personal journey as a caregiver for Sharen and wonderfully connects his unexpected life experiences and his 27 years in broadcast media to leadership insights. Ross' core values of family and faith are strongly reflected in how he approached life challenges and pursued new career opportunities to help individuals strengthen leadership development. You will take away key strategies in improving your leadership skills while assessing new approaches in working with, growing and investing in your team."*

*Tim Daman*
*President & CEO*
*Lansing Regional Chamber of Commerce*

*"A leadership book with a twist. Ross Woodstock uses narratives not only about his own personal leadership journey, but others that offer a window into his wife's perseverance as she rises to meet the challenges of her new health reality. Ross learns to navigate those waters with her and offers us personal insight on how that impacted him in ways he never expected. In learning to look at life differently, Ross developed twelve leadership principles and a road map for personal development. Those principles, paired with actionable items, guide you through your own leadership journey. Since reading Ross' book, I have already put his principles into practice, and I am a better leader because of it. This is a must-read."*

*Sheri Jones*
*News Anchor*
*WLNS-TV, WLAJ-TV*

"Ross Woodstock has managed to capture the traits and skills required of both caregivers and leaders and masterfully unite them in one of the most compelling and insightful leadership books I've read. This type of revelation only comes from someone who has experienced pain, passion, purpose and divine inspiration. It is a must-read for leaders and the more than 38 million unpaid family caregivers."

*Paula D. Cunningham*

"It's the rare voice one finds in leadership circles and especially in leadership writing—one inspired by real experience, heartfelt love and an enduring strength—that while sorrowful, finds a reason to rejoice. Ross Woodstock takes us through a journey that we will not soon forget. It's one thing to write a book about leadership. It's another to demonstrate sincere leadership within one's inner person. This book is for those who are ready to embrace leadership at a personal and professional level. Not just read about leadership—but to truly embrace the journey into leadership."

*Justin M. Sheehan*
*Executive Director*
*Lansing Promise Foundation*

# DEDICATION

*To Sharen A. Woodstock, my hero and inspiration.*

# ACKNOWLEDGEMENTS

First and foremost, I want to thank God who makes all things possible. I praise Him for giving me the wisdom, strength, diligence, patience, resources and encouragement I needed to write this book.

I am blessed with an amazing family and am so thankful for Sharen—my wife, best friend and the mother of our children. Our two amazing children, Michael and Nicole, have made life fulfilling and fun.

I have been fortunate to work with many leaders who have richly influenced my career. Thanks to Gary (Duke) Williams, the late Robert Ditmer, Art Wainwright, Elaine Blakeley, Tim Skubick, the late Howard Lancour, the late Ronald Kwasnick and the late Grant Santimore. I would not be where I am today without the opportunities and wisdom these leaders shared with me.

I would like to thank fellow authors Dr. David Chinsky, Brad Mitchell and Chris Johnson who so generously offered their time and support during this process. I am also most appreciative of the time that many friends dedicated to reviewing the manuscript and offering thoughtful suggestions, including; Tim Daman, Sheri Jones, Paula Cunningham, Justin Sheehan and Ray Tadgerson.

Many thanks to Robert Kolt and the team at Kolt Communications who are the best group of colleagues ever.

I also have been fortunate to have the greatest group of clients over the years who have enriched me in so many ways. A special thanks to my coaching clients who gave permission to share part of their stories in the telling of this book.

# TABLE OF CONTENTS

INTRODUCTION ........................ 11

LEADERSHIP INSIGHT #1:
BUILD A STRONG FOUNDATION OF VALUES ............... 17
Values Are Your Guiding Light ...................... 20
How to Identify Your Values .............. 22
Live Your Values as a Leader ............ 23
When Team Values Break Down ................... 25

LEADERSHIP INSIGHT #2:
IT IS NOT ABOUT YOU ......................... 30
The Four Most Powerful Words in Leadership ................ 32
I BELIEVE IN YOU. ............... 33
The Results of Investing Yourself into Others ............ 34
How to Invest Yourself into Others ............... 38

LEADERSHIP INSIGHT #3:
CELEBRATE THE SMALL MILESTONES ............. 44
Be Intentional About Celebrating Small Milestones ............ 46
The Benefits of Celebrations .............. 48
How to Celebrate Small Milestones with Your Team ........... 50

LEADERSHIP INSIGHT #4:
DISCOVER THE POWER OF POSITIVITY ............ 53
Positivity Overcomes Negativity ............... 54
Negative Voices Are All Around Us .............. 56
Internal Voices Can Be Most Damaging ............. 57

Positive Leadership Drives Positive Organizational Results .......... 58

Maintaining a Positive Culture ................................................ 59

## LEADERSHIP INSIGHT #5:
## MAINTAIN AN ATTITUDE OF GRATITUDE ...................... 62

Is the Glass Half-Empty or Half-Full? ..................................... 64

The Science on Gratitude ....................................................... 65

The Story of My Christmas Tie ............................................... 66

Expressing Gratitude ............................................................. 67

Appreciate What Others Bring to Your Team ........................... 68

You Reap What You Sow ........................................................ 70

## LEADERSHIP INSIGHT #6:
## HUMILITY IS THE ULTIMATE STRENGTH ...................... 72

Humble Pie with a Side of In-Your-Face ................................. 74

The Importance of Humility on the Team ............................... 76

Leadership That Models Humility .......................................... 78

How to be a Humble Leader .................................................. 80

## LEADERSHIP INSIGHT #7:
## EMPATHY - WALK A MILE IN THEIR SHOES .................. 83

We're Losing It ...................................................................... 85

Get Out of Your Bubble ........................................................ 89

A Culture of Empathy Breeds Trust, Communication, Creative
Problem Solving & Innovation ............................................... 91

Building a Culture of Empathy .............................................. 94

## LEADERSHIP INSIGHT #8:
## ENCOURAGE THE COURAGE IN OTHERS ...................... 98

Encouragement and Its Profound Impact on History ................. 99

Leaders Must Show the Way .................................................. 100

Encourage Through Affirmation ................................... 102

Encourage Their Confidence ...................................... 104

Encourage through Failure ........................................ 106

Empower and Trust ................................................ 107

Encourage the Courage Across the Finish Line ................... 108

## LEADERSHIP INSIGHT # 9:
## OVERCOME LIFE'S CHALLENGES WITH RESILIENCE 110

Tough Times are an Opportunity for Growth ..................... 112

Don't Bounce Back. Bounce Forward ............................. 116

Tough Times are an Opportunity to Pull People Together ........ 117

Take Care of Yourself ............................................. 119

Keep Things in Perspective ...................................... 122

Develop a Resilient Crisis Plan .................................. 124

## LEADERSHIP INSIGHT #10:
## DEVELOP EVERYONE TO THEIR FULLEST
## POTENTIAL .................................................... 126

Recognizing Potential in Others ................................. 128

Developing Others is Good Business .............................. 129

Why Development Does Not Happen ................................. 130

Build a People First Culture ..................................... 132

Putting Development into Action ................................. 134

## LEADERSHIP INSIGHT #11:
## LIVE YOUR LEADERSHIP LEGACY EVERY DAY ............. 140

Why Leaders Should Care About Their Legacy ..................... 141

Connecting to Your "Why" ........................................ 147

Create Your Legacy Statement .................................... 149

Live Your Legacy ................................................................ 151

Seize Your Moments of Courage ....................................... 153

LEADERSHIP INSIGHT #12:
CHART YOUR JOURNEY ON TRANSFORMATION
HIGHWAY ........................................................................156

Transformation Highway is Filled with Potholes .............. 158

Continuous Learning Fosters Transformation ................... 161

Transformation Over the Next Decade .............................. 163

Transform the World One Leader at a Time ...................... 165

The Transformation Journey Requires Daily Focus ........... 167

SHOCKING STATISTICS ABOUT CAREGIVING ............170

ENDNOTES ......................................................................174

ABOUT THE AUTHOR ...................................................180

# Lead to Lift Up Others

*Leadership Insights from a Caregiver's Journey*

# Introduction

"This doesn't look good."

Those words pierced my soul.

They were spoken by one of the paramedics who were in the den of our home trying to revive my wife, Sharen. She was not in bed when I woke up at 4 a.m. on Friday, September 21, 2007. That was not unusual in itself. However, what I discovered when I walked into the den was most unusual. Sharen was sitting in front of the computer. It took me a minute to realize that she was not responsive and something was seriously wrong.

The next several hours were a surreal blur of events: an ambulance ride where I prayed over Sharen and desperately urged her to wake up; calls to our two children to meet me in the emergency room at Sparrow Hospital; a flurry of medical personnel and a battery of tests; uncertainty over whether Sharen would live and an emergency room doctor suggesting that even if she survived, her quality of life was very much in question; calls to family and friends; and the slow, agonizing awakening to a new reality in which I realized no matter the outcome, life was never going to be the same.

Sharen had suffered a stroke. Contributing factors included undiagnosed high blood pressure, diabetes and carotid arteries that were almost 100 percent blocked. Sharen underwent successful surgery to place a stent in one of her carotid arteries, which provided hope for her recovery.

The next two weeks at Sparrow Hospital featured an endless procession of medical tests, doctors asking the same questions and an incredible group of therapists who patiently and expertly worked with Sharen—encouraging her to speak, helping her to sit up and monitoring movement on the right side of her body, which as it turned out had been permanently compromised. I am forever grateful for the amazing team of medical professionals who cared for her.

During those two weeks, I spent 23 hours a day at the hospital with just one hour per day to go home, shower and change. I made no complaints. After all, I realized Sharen didn't have that opportunity. As difficult as this period in our lives seemed at the time, I did not understand the magnitude of the challenges that lay ahead.

Sharen was forced to endure six-and-a-half weeks in a rehabilitation center, a move that was required by the insurance company. She hated every minute there. The food was awful, the quality of care was inconsistent at best, and the environment—well, it wasn't quite the same as the neurology unit at the hospital. Fortunately, the therapists there were top-notch, and Sharen continued to make enough progress so she eventually was able to return home.

The transition from hospital to rehabilitation center and eventually to our home was a stark wake-up call for me. I spent about 14 hours a day at the rehabilitation center and slowly got myself back to the office a few hours a day for work. The combination of Sharen's intense desire to go home (a transition for which she was nowhere near ready), the pressure of insurance company mandates (are you starting to see a pattern here?) that required me to rapidly—and at considerable out-of-pocket expense—prepare our home for her eventual return, and the necessity to provide quality service to my clients at work was overwhelming.

During that period, I started to understand the new normal in my life.

I was a caregiver.

I was totally unprepared to serve in this role. Truth be told, I wasn't even wired for this role.

Me. A caregiver. For real?

Sharen endured months of therapy, first at home and later as an outpatient. Eventually, she was able to walk short distances with a walker. It hasn't been easy. Sharen is a fiercely independent person who is used to setting her own schedule. She can no longer drive, and her inability to navigate steps makes it nearly impossible to visit friends. She has faced numerous other health issues since her stroke, including a battle with cancer.

Those who know Sharen are aware of her overwhelmingly positive attitude towards life. She has approached each and every challenge with an unbelievable level of optimism. Sharen has always loved serving her family and has learned to manage the cooking, cleaning and home management issues that she has always enjoyed. (Well, she hates cleaning but does like the fact that she is able to handle many of those unpleasantries). To put it quite simply, Sharen is an inspiration to all of us who are blessed to have her in our lives.

For me, the journey as a caregiver has been one of trial and error—somedays it seems mostly error. I often have joked with Sharen that when it comes to caregiving, what I lack in talent, I make up for with love. She likes to say she has the best help she can afford.

After more than a decade as a caregiver, I came to a realization: I LIKE BEING A CAREGIVER. That may seem like an odd statement to make. Especially from someone like me. I don't believe anybody aspires to become a loved one's caregiver. However, it is a role in which many of us find ourselves at some point in our lives.

Being a caregiver has transformed my life. I am not the same person I was on September 21, 2007. Caregiving has changed me in many ways that I will write about in this book. I have become a person who puts others before myself (not always, but I am getting better). My pride has been overtaken by humility. I have a deeper understanding of what love is all about. I have become more patient (again, nowhere near perfection on that one), and I find joy in bringing joy to others. Transformation is a life-long process. I am nowhere near the person I should be, but my role as a caregiver has brought me quite a long way on the transformation journey.

In my work as an executive coach and leadership consultant, I help leaders achieve sustainable growth in their careers. I have long considered writing a book about leadership. As I was pondering potential topics, it occurred to me that my role as a caregiver has taught me more about leadership than anything else in my life. To be quite honest, caregiving has taught me more about leadership than all of the books, courses, degrees, certifications and trainings I have been privileged to experience.

The need for outstanding leaders is more pressing than ever. The massive exodus of baby boomers from the workplace has drained organizational culture of experience and leadership expertise that takes years to replace. Those who remain in the workforce face the constant reality of having to do more with less. Technology now has us plugged into our global society 24/7, which creates constant demand for our attention and time. The notion of work/life balance is nothing more than a fleeting fantasy for most. In the midst of this harried, stressful environment, there is a desperate need for strong leaders. Leaders who can rise above the challenges of the 21st century workplace and bring diverse teams and ideas together for the common good. Leaders who can coax the best out of others and show that they genuinely care about each team member. Leaders who are willing to invest in the development and fulfillment of those around them.

One of the leadership lessons that took the longest to sink in for me was this realization: My work as a leader is not about me. It's true. *Your work as a leader is not about you.* It is about what we as leaders should be doing to lift up others around us. Our leadership should be built around lifting up our direct reports, out peers, even our bosses. If you dedicate your leadership life to lifting up others, you will find that people will prosper and grow, teams will be stronger, more cohesive and productive and the organization will flourish. People want to work for and with leaders who focus their energy on lifting up others. Your career will be more satisfying and fulfilling when you lead to lift up others.

Throughout this book, you will find principles you can employ to help you be that kind of leader. I will share insights into the leadership lessons I've learned in my role as a caregiver. I will share some of my personal stories, but more importantly, I will connect those lessons to your work as a leader, in whatever capacity you serve. At the end of each chapter, you will find coaching tips. These are practical, real-world ways you can apply these leadership lessons in your everyday work as a leader. If you are willing to go the extra mile, you will find these helpful tips to be difference-makers in your leadership career.

I am confident that if you apply this book's principles in your life, your leadership abilities will reach heights you never dreamed possible. This transformation will lead you to experience the same rich, rewarding and fulfilling existence that I have enjoyed during the best years of my life—as a caregiver!

# Build a Strong Foundation of Values

*"When you achieve complete congruence between your values and your goals, like a hand in a glove, you feel strong, happy, healthy, and fully integrated as a person. You develop a kind of courage that makes you completely unafraid to make decisions and take action. Your whole life improves when you begin living your life by the values that you most admire."—Brian Tracy*

Nothing in my life prepared me for my role as a caregiver. The early months were the most stressful days of my life. Over the years, I had dealt with the loss of loved ones, financial struggles and emotional upheaval. I even survived puberty! Those turbulent times did not compare with being thrust into caregiving.

The care and support Sharen and I received at Sparrow Hospital was incredible. However, I quickly began to awaken to a stark reality: We were about to be forced into a system that was stacked against us.

The first dose of bad news was even though Sharen could not sit up in bed without assistance, she was going to be discharged from the hospital and would have to be admitted to a rehabilitation center. I was dumbfounded at the thought that a patient clearly in need of long-term care was so quickly kicked to the curb. The medical professionals explained to me that insurance companies make the decision as to how long a patient can remain in the hospital—and according to our insurance company, her time was up.

Shortly thereafter, we received the second dose of bad news. As I began to hurriedly research the rehab centers in our area, I discovered the best facilities did not accept private pay insurance because those centers don't want to jump through the "hoops" required by those insurance companies. Consequently, I was limited to a choice of just three homes. After completing a tour of the first home, my daughter broke down into tears at the thought of her mother having to endure a single hour in that disaster zone.

We were fortunate that the best of the three facilities available to us did, in fact, admit Sharen. As it turns out, it was a mixed blessing. The physical and occupational therapy facilities and staff were very good, something for which I will always be incredibly grateful. The rest of the experience—well, not so much. The care was inconsistent at best, especially overnight when staffing was kept at the state minimum levels, and the food was simply awful. Sharen was understandably miserable and insisted daily that I take her home. The problem was she wasn't physically ready to live at home, and I wasn't emotionally prepared.

At this point, I had returned to work. The stress of trying to run my business and spend as many hours a day as possible with Sharen quickly began to take its toll. Additionally, I faced constant pressure knowing the insurance company could determine it would discontinue payments for the nursing home stay—in which case, Sharen probably would be discharged, whether we were ready or not.

In order to prepare for Sharen's discharge, I had to invest in significant alterations to our home and get those projects completed quickly. Sharen's two brothers built a wheelchair ramp so I could get her in and out of the house. I also had to have four doorways widened to allow for wheelchair access and have two sliding glass doors removed to set-up a bedroom for her, which also meant acquiring a hospital bed. Additionally, I had to interview and hire a caregiving company to provide staff at our home when I would be at work. Sharen would require someone in the house 24/7 for several months. Of course, none of these costs were covered by insurance, and it all had to be completed in a few short weeks.

The stress became so overwhelming, it was almost unbearable. There were two occasions when I literally felt like I was going to collapse. The second time, I was certain I was having a nervous breakdown. I was alone at my office early on a Friday morning when the world started to cave-in. As I felt seconds from crashing, I closed my office door and lay face down on the floor. At that moment, I called on my Christian faith and cried out, "God, please save me!"

You can interpret what happened next however you'd like. I believe it was God's power that picked me up off that floor and filled me with energy. There was no way I could have survived that moment with my own strength alone. In my mind, without a doubt, it was a supernatural act that saved me from a serious medical catastrophe—which would have had dire consequences for both me and Sharen.

What saved me at that pivotal moment was the fact that I have a strong foundation of values. In difficult times, I turn to these values. They guide me in how I live my life and influence every decision and action that I take. Just as you need values to guide you in everyday life, as a leader you must have values that serve as the foundation for how you lead.

# VALUES ARE YOUR GUIDING LIGHT

Every decision you make in life is rooted in your core values. They guide your behavior and the choices you make. If integrity is one of your core values, and you find yourself facing an ethical question, you are likely to make a decision that takes you down a path that is moral and just.

This brings an important history lesson to mind. As the Civil War drew to a close and a Union victory became apparent, President Abe Lincoln recognized it was time to heal the wounds of the war. Lincoln knew that to achieve peace and true national unity, there must be reconciliation. People expected Lincoln to use his second inaugural address in 1864 to celebrate the impending Union victory. Instead, he unexpectedly shifted directions and turned to a startling conclusion: "With malice toward none, with charity to all," Lincoln was calling on the nation to move into a new era—an era not imbued with retribution, but one filled with forgiveness and harmony. Lincoln's ability to convince the nation to support reconciliation was likely due to the fact that people admired his values and trusted him as a leader. How had Lincoln earned such a high level of trust? It all came down to his values—values from which he never wavered and always clearly communicated, whether in letters or casual communications. Following his last meeting with the president, shortly before Lincoln was assassinated, General William Sherman reflected on these characteristics when he wrote: "Of all the men I have met, he seemed to possess more of the elements of greatness, combined with goodness, than any other."

Staying anchored in your values brings fulfillment and meaning into your life. As a young man, I aspired to have a career in broadcast journalism. I started my career working at a tiny radio station in St. Johns, Michigan. It was a wonderful opportunity to learn the business from the ground-up. I started my own little news and sports department, interviewing local newsmakers and high school coaches. I even had the opportunity to do sports play-by-play for high school football and basketball. I was living the dream!

Though the job was fulfilling, challenging and most definitely a lot of fun, Sharen and I were struggling financially. For the first couple of years, I worked part-time with no benefits. Eventually I became a full-time employee with health insurance, but we were living paycheck to paycheck and having a hard time making ends meet. I attempted to land a higher paying broadcast journalism job in a larger market, but I quickly became frustrated. I felt that I was being unfairly passed over in job interviews. It seemed like my dream career was turning into a nightmare.

Just as our frustrations were reaching a peak, I was offered an opportunity to move into a potentially lucrative new career as a travelling salesman for a popular sporting goods line. I faced a crossroads in my life: Do I take the path that offers more immediate financial security for my family? Or do I give my dream career one final shot—even though I had no new job prospects?

Ultimately, I chose the career that gave me a sense of purpose and meaning over the one that offered me more money. Why? Because this was the choice that most aligned with my personal values—and the decision ended up paying off in spades. A few weeks after turning down the sporting goods sales career, I was offered a job at the number one radio station in Lansing, Michigan. This position became the springboard for a wonderful, highly successful career in radio and television that lasted for more than two decades.

## HOW TO IDENTIFY YOUR VALUES

In my work as an executive coach, I often start my one-on-one coaching engagements by asking my clients to identify their core values. I have found this useful in a number of ways. First of all, it allows the client to focus on what it is really important in their life. Secondly, it serves as a connecting point for us during the coaching engagement. When the client is considering potential action steps they might take, I will often ask them to consider how each action step aligns with their core values.

You will find that considering your values foundation is time well spent. A simple, but effective technique is to identify your top 10 to 15 values. Once you have completed that list, identify the top three. Lastly, select your number one most important value. Keep your list of values on hand and reflect on it from time-to-time.

In his book *What Matters Most* (Franklin Covey 2000), author Hyrum W. Smith recommends what he calls the "Why Drill" to refine your list of values. For each value, ask yourself a series of why questions and make notes about the answers, such as:

- Why do I spend so much time with this person, activity or thing?
- Why do I feel so strongly about this value?
- Why do I spend money on things related to this value?

- Why am I pouring so much energy into this project, relationship or activity?
- Why do I spend so little time or energy on this value? (1)

Continue to drill down and ask "why" questions until you are satisfied that the value truly belongs on your list.

If you prefer a more scientific approach, there are a number of tools available that you can tap into if you want to dig deep into identifying your core values. My favorite free assessment is the Via Survey of Character Strengths, which is available at www.viacharacter.org.

The point is that you must have a strong foundation of values that will serve as the basis of all the decisions you make, how you live your life and how you relate to others in your work as a leader. When you need it the most, these values will be your rock-solid foundation and guiding light.

## LIVE YOUR VALUES AS A LEADER

I recently worked with a team that was struggling with a number of issues. Their greatest challenges were a low level of trust, breakdowns in communications and a number of interpersonal conflicts, all of which were making the team unproductive and quite miserable. The team-building program that we walked through together was a slow, arduous and often frustrating experience for all of us. Frankly, I began to doubt that this team would ever turn things in a positive direction.

Just as things were looking particularly bleak for the team, an employee who had been a distraction decided to leave the organization. I was holding my breath to see how the rest of the team would react. To my delight, the remaining team members viewed the departure as an opportunity to take their group in a new, positive direction. They decided to start by identifying core values for their organization. I facilitated discussions with them that eventually resulted in their agreement on five or six core values.

The team was quite proud of the breakthrough they had made, and understandably so. They talked about how to display their new values for all the world to see. Perhaps they would post them on the wall in their office. They also discussed having laminated cards printed that they would carry with them and hand out to their customers. They asked me what I thought about those ideas. My answer shocked them.

"Both of those ideas are very nice, and if you want to do them, go right ahead," I said, "But at the end of the day, neither one means anything."

A stunned silence fell over the room. How could I—someone who is typically an encouraging facilitator—basically throw cold water on them and ruin their momentum? How deflating!

I followed up with actionable advice: "What matters most is how well you live these values every day. Sure, you can display them on the wall, but unless you are intentional about putting your values into action, they will be nothing more than an attractive decoration." With this, the team developed a deeper understanding of the importance of values—and this allowed them to continue down their path to a more positive future.

Computer software company Adobe has received great notoriety for its culture. One of Adobe's core values revolves around encouraging innovation. The company has won awards for its Kickbox program, which empowers team members to develop new ideas. As part of this program, when a staff member requests it, Adobe gives them a red carboard box and $1,000 prepaid credit card to explore their idea. Many of these ideas ultimately have been developed to the point that they received further investment from Adobe.

Living your values is not something you should do by accident. Develop specific strategies that effectively hardwire your values into your corporate DNA. FreshBooks is another company that put programs in place that aligned with their corporate values. To live out their value of empathy, the company started a "blind date" program to help new employees get to know others around the company. They also do a "heads-up hello," in which employees learn each other's names and make eye contact when they say hello. (2)

In the workplace of the 21st century knowledge economy, it's particularly critical to be a leader who drives your team to live out the organization's core values. Millennials and Gen Z now make up more than half of the workforce. These younger generations are insisting that their employers have a much higher sense of social responsibility than in past decades. People in today's workforce want to be part of organizations that are committed to making the office a better place. If you want to be a successful leader in today's workplace, you must live your life on a foundation of strong values and inspire those around you to intentionally put the core values of your team into action every day.

## WHEN TEAM VALUES BREAK DOWN

When employees are engaged, they wholeheartedly adopt the vision and values of their organization. One of the most damaging developments on any team is when employees become disengaged. The negative impact of disengagement cannot be overstated. It hurts productivity, morale and retention. According to numerous studies, the financial cost attributed to disengagement is astronomical.

There are many reasons why employees become disengaged—from lack of challenge, laziness or apathy or a lack of initiative to unhealthy habits, lack of development opportunities, limited advancement and poor leadership. Oftentimes, the root cause of disengagement is the simple fact that an employee is not connected to your organization's values. There could be many reasons why this occurs: Your values may not motivate them to perform; they may not be clear on what the values are and how they should be connected to them; or they may not know how to align with your team's values. There are a number of steps you can take to help those team members connect with and live out your values:

### Step #1: Clearly communicate the mission, vision and values.

In many cases, team members simply don't have a firm grasp on the organization's mission, vision and values. I often offer training for teams in this area, ensuring that all the employees currently working there are connecting and aligning with the organization's core values. What about folks who are hired later? It is critical to educate these new employees and ensure there are ongoing communications about values with the entire team. After all, this is your culture. It addresses how team members treat each other, customers and other stakeholders. This can make or break your company.

A few years ago, I attended a presentation by the CEO of the Grand Traverse Pie Company. Before his presentation, I said hello to him and welcomed him to our community. He immediately asked me my name, which I found a bit unusual. During his presentation, he talked about the organization's 16 core values. He told the crowd that each day, the company identifies one of the core values and expects all employees to give special attention to that particular value. On the day of his speech, the core value in focus was knowing everyone's name. What a terrific approach to not only living out core values, but also getting all team members more connected to those values.

## Step #2: Help team members clarify what is important to them.

From time to time, you will have team members who aren't connected to the company's values because those values may not be as important to them personally. This is a good time for some coaching conversations with your employee.

Find out what motivates them. What are they passionate about? After digging deeper, you may determine that they simply aren't in the right job position at the company. It benefits you and the employee to come to this understanding. In some cases, you may be able to shift them to another position. Based on your conversations, you may also conclude that this employee just is not a good fit with your team. Better to reach these understandings together than to continue along with a disgruntled, disengaged employee.

## Step #3: Make disconnected employees feel like part of the team.

Some people aren't connected to the team because they just don't know how. They could be introverts who need a little extra encouragement. Many young people, especially those in their first job, have never been taught what being in the workplace is all about and how to integrate with a team.

You may consider developing a mentoring program, which can be especially powerful for teaching new employees all the tips they need to be successful in their job. Organize periodic team building activities such as community service projects, fun bonding activities and trainings that help people get to know and understand their teammates. It is important for everyone to understand that we are all wired differently, and some folks need more help than others when it comes to making connections in the workplace.

## Step #4: Let them know how they are doing.

Regular feedback is essential. Hopefully, you offer employee feedback at least quarterly if not more frequently. I am amazed at how often workers are not meeting expectations and nobody bothers to tell them.

Author Patrick Lencioni tells the story about his own struggles with holding people accountable. He had a manager leading a project who was not meeting expectations. Pat and one of the other managers decided to hold a meeting and explain to this project manager how he was falling short. The project manager thanked Pat and his colleague for telling him the truth and said, "Throughout my career, nobody has ever told me I wasn't performing up to standards. I never would have known if you hadn't said something." Lencioni says the manager's performance in future weeks went "through the roof." All because of the willingness of his colleagues to have a difficult conversation at the right time. (3)

An organization is known by its employees. Your values set the standard for a work environment where all team members coexist and hopefully flourish. Good values are essential to promote positivity, strong work ethic and integrity. They also connect your team members to the organization's purpose and focus employees on working towards a common goal. Additionally, these values serve as the pillar on which growth can occur, and they are what allow organizations to attract and retain great talent.

## COACHING TIPS

**Coaching Tip #1:** Draft a list of 10 to 15 personal core values. Reflect on your choices. Identify your top three. Then, select your number one value. Keep your list of values and refer to it regularly.

**Coaching Tip #2:** Make values discussions a regular part of team meetings. Set aside time at least once quarterly to share thoughts on how your team is living out your values. Ask what new approaches would help you take the team's values commitment to the next level.

# LEADERSHIP INSIGHT #2:

# It Is Not About You

*"True leaders understand that leadership is not about them but about those they serve. It is not about exalting themselves but about lifting others up."—Sheri L. Dew*

Caregiving is a rewarding and fulfilling role. Of course, it also comes with its challenges. In fact, I have found there are more potholes on the road of caregiving than you'd find on a typical Michigan road— and believe me that is *a lot* of potholes!

One day, I was sharing some of my caregiving experiences with my pastor, who is also a dear friend of mine. During the course of the conversation, I remarked (not in a complaining way) about how much of a challenge some of those experiences were for me.

"Not to mention what those experiences mean for Sharen," responded the pastor.

Oh yeah—Sharen.

I felt mildly embarrassed about the self-centered nature of my comments. I was failing to focus on the importance of investing myself into my wife's life. Instead, I was focusing on how I personally was being impacted by the caregiving experience.

Often in life, we have a tendency to frame our thoughts and actions around our own desires, goals, agendas and judgments. In the professional world, this "me-centered" attitude can sabotage a leader's career; and more often than not, it leads to a work culture that lacks trust, engagement and esprit de corps, which will quickly derail any team.

I recently was hired by an organization's board of directors to figure out why the company had experienced a rash of top executives leaving for other jobs. As I interviewed numerous team members, it quickly became apparent that trust was nonexistent within the organization— and the source of the breakdown appeared to be the CEO.

As I dug deeper, I discovered an e-mail the CEO had sent to her leadership team imploring them to achieve their annual goals so she could qualify for her bonus. During a subsequent meeting that included myself, the CEO and one of her direct reports, the CEO told her team member that she didn't plan on staying with this company for a long time, so she needed to push her agenda forward aggressively in order to facilitate her career advancement. This leader was making the work of the organization all about herself, which was deflating and demoralizing the team and causing a mass exodus of great talent.

Leadership is not about you as the leader. It is about your team. Your focus should not be your own career advancement, but that of others. If you want your team to realize its full potential, they need to know that you care deeply about their growth, their dreams, their success and their happiness.

When you invest your time and efforts into the success of others, you are adding value into their lives. Adding value is, in a sense, an intentional act of making a deposit into the life of another. The more deposits you make, the bigger the return on your investment—whether it is the growth and success of your work team, new opportunities that come along or the strengthening of your marriage and family. Leaders add value by using their skills and expertise to guide, nurture, counsel, encourage, inspire, affirm and challenge individuals at work, at home and in their community. As the saying goes, a rising tide floats all boats. If we help others grow stronger, everyone wins!

## THE FOUR MOST POWERFUL WORDS IN LEADERSHIP

Throughout my career, I have had the privilege to work for and alongside some great leaders, and I have been blessed to learn some impactful lessons from these individuals. (I'll admit, I have also learned more than a few things as the result of my own missteps along the way.) I am eternally grateful to a number of people who gave me opportunities to prove myself. One of the greatest leadership lessons I learned during the early years of my career was the importance of four little words in our lives.

I call them the four most powerful words in leadership.

They are simple words, really. But the cumulative effect of these words on an organization, a community and, yes, even the world, can be amazing. If you live by these words every day—not just memorize them and say them, but truly live them out in your own leadership life—these four words will make a significant difference in your ability to make a difference in your organization, your ability to build great teams, your ability to build a stronger, more profitable business, and most importantly your ability to make a difference in the lives of those around you.

These are the four most powerful words in leadership:

# I BELIEVE IN YOU.

*I believe in you.* There is nothing more powerful you can do or say to inspire, encourage and motivate those around you than simply letting them know you believe in them. Let them know that you are on their side; that you are willing to go the extra mile to help them achieve their dreams; that what is important to them is important to you; that you are willing to give them a chance to try new things; and that you are willing to challenge them to achieve things maybe they didn't even think were possible.

Every person we know, every person on our work teams, everyone in our lives—including you and me—has a huge reservoir of untapped potential. By believing in others, we can help people unleash that potential, making them more productive, more effective and more fulfilled.

Sometimes, we can say the simplest things to people, but it has a major impact. As a young radio reporter, I had the privilege of covering the Michigan State Capitol. It was a terrific experience. I was challenged daily as I learned to break down complex government issues in a way that was understandable for the audience, tell stories and present information accurately and fairly and work at a very fast pace.

At the end of each year, I had the opportunity to have a one-on-one sit-down interview with the Michigan Governor, William Milliken. It was one of my favorite tasks. Governor Milliken was a very smooth, polished politician who could handle anything I threw his way. I always asked a few tough questions in an effort to break through the rhetoric and get a deeper understanding of issues. One year, I was conducting my interview with Governor Milliken late on a Friday afternoon. It was the last thing both of us were doing before heading home for the weekend. As I was packing up and he was pulling his overcoat out of the closet, he looked at me and said:

"You are very good at what you do."

That was it. A simple sentence. It was one of the most encouraging things anyone had ever said to me. The fact that I remember this statement 40 years later speaks to the impact it had on my life. I never covered Governor Milliken any differently, but I always had the highest level of respect for the work he did, the quality of person he was and the positive contribution he made in my career.

*I believe in you.*

Four little words. They can make all the difference. If you are willing to look beyond what others see and dig a little deeper, you will recognize the true potential in others. By letting them know you believe in them, you will help them unleash their talent and break through the barriers that that have been holding them back.

## THE RESULTS OF INVESTING YOURSELF INTO OTHERS

When you make an ongoing, conscious effort to invest yourself into others, you will see a significant return on that investment. You and your team will experience a bounty of benefits, both short-term and long-term.

Robert Greenleaf is the father of modern-day servant leadership. A retired AT&T executive, Greenleaf wrote that servant leaders are servants first who make certain that the needs of others are their highest priority.

> *"The best test, and difficult to administer, is this: Do those served grow as persons? Do they, while being served, become healthier, wiser, freer, more autonomous, more likely themselves to become servants?"—Robert Greenleaf (1)*

When you practice servant leadership and invest in others, you will enjoy an array of valuable results:

### #1: Investing in others shifts your focus.

I have great admiration for my many friends who work in the non-profit sector. The financial rewards are not as great as the private sector and the demands of raising funds to provide adequate services is more challenging than ever. I admire the passion of those who work to serve those in need. What encourages people in the non-profit arena to come back to work every day? I believe it's the reward of knowing they have made a difference in the lives of those they serve.

During my early years as a communications strategist, I was hired to manage communications for the local chapter of Habitat for Humanity when the Jimmy Carter Work Project (JCWP) came to our community. Over a period of several months, JCWP built several homes for families in our area. When construction was completed and families were ready to move into the new homes, we planned a big media day. During this event, we held a ribbon-cutting at four different homes around the city.

I was blown away to see how much those homes meant to a diverse group of families who otherwise would not have been able to afford such a home. They were low income families, some single parents, some immigrants, and all very proud of what they could accomplish in life. The happiness on their faces filled my heart with joy. This is the joy you will experience when you focus your leadership on investing in the careers of those around you.

## #2: Investing in others is contagious.

I often tell leaders to focus on what they can control and work on changing the world one person at a time. Whenever you engage in a positive behavior, you are modeling that behavior for others. Others will notice as you achieve success, and your efforts may soon start to spread organically throughout the organization.

We all have had the experience of dealing with idiot drivers on the highway. The natural reaction is to get angry and maybe seek revenge. Bob Hoffman had those feelings for a moment when a driver cut him off on the road—but instead of staying angry, he was inspired to launch a movement eventually known as ePIFanyNow™. Bob's idea was to encourage people to commit random acts of kindness and pass it forward.

The movement spread quickly, and now Bob's annual "pass it forward" events draw hundreds of people who share and celebrate the power of kindness. Annual awards are presented to young people who have taken up special causes—including a group of kids who raised thousands of dollars for a young neighbor with a rare neuro-muscular disorder, a young girl whose "Suitcases for Kids" program collects clothes and supplies for foster children, and a boy who gained national attention for a thank you party he hosted for police officers, whom he felt were unduly criticized by the media.

As a leader, when you let people know they matter to you by investing yourself into them, you build a culture where passing it forward becomes part of the program. That contagious culture will encourage excellence at all levels, and employees will sacrifice their individual agendas for the good of the team.

## #3: Investing in others helps attract and retain great talent.

Organizations in the 21$^{st}$ century knowledge economy are in a battle for the best talent. There are more jobs than are there are people to fill those jobs. This places the talent in the driver's seat when it comes to choosing where they want to work.

Emergent BioSolutions is a manufacturer headquartered in Bethesda, Maryland with a facility in Lansing, Michigan. Emergent has a well-developed coaching program in which employees volunteer to participate. Employees must go through a training program to become certified as coaches. Coaches have the opportunity to coach employees working in departments other than their own.

Not only has this program been an asset as an individual development tool, but the inter-departmental nature of the coaching relationships has promoted greater understanding and harmony throughout the organization. As a high-level research and development organization, Emergent regularly recruits scientists who are in demand across the country. It can be a challenge to convince someone with a PhD to relocate to Lansing, Michigan as opposed to competing opportunities on the east or west coast. Emergent has found that the company's coaching program and emphasis on developing talent has been a difference-maker in their ability to recruit the best talent to their organization.

## #4: Investing in others increases engagement.

The companies with the highest level of employee engagement are the ones that develop their talent. Employees want the opportunity to grow, learn new skills and continue to get better at what they do. This is particularly true of millennials. On average, millennials stay in a job for just 19 months. In other words, companies are not working hard enough to retain millennial talent.

Now, we have Gen Z coming into the workplace. These workers have different influences, but they share the desire to work for an organization where leaders invest in their people. To avoid the high cost of turnover, organizations must relate to this talent and make sure employees know their leaders care about their growth. When leaders invest themselves into Gen Z and millennial workers, this increases engagement and greatly improves employee retention rates.

## #5: Investing in others delivers results.

There is ample research that supports the notion that a more engaged workforce has a direct positive impact on the bottom line. An engaged employee is much more likely to be in alignment with the goals of the organization, and they will work harder and produce better results. Teams full of engaged employees are more cohesive and productive, they make better, faster decisions and they put the team goals ahead of their own personal ambitions. As software executive Jim Goodnight says, "If you treat your employees like they make a difference, they will." (2)

## HOW TO INVEST YOURSELF INTO OTHERS

The greatest and most effective leaders all share something in common: They commit to investing their skills, expertise and wisdom into those around them. However, there is no question that investing in others requires a significant time commitment. Perhaps this is why many well-intentioned leaders get derailed when it comes time to put theory into action.

I counsel leaders in my coaching practice to implement anything new in manageable steps. Start small. Do one thing, and do it really well. Then, move on to the next goal. Over time, you will find that you have been able to incorporate these techniques into your everyday work as a leader. That is when you will really start to notice results.

Here are five ways you can invest yourself into others:

### #1: Listen to them.

This sounds like a no-brainer, but listening is something that easily gets swept aside in the hustle and bustle of our everyday lives. Listening takes time, and time is something we don't have a whole lot of these days. As leaders, our lives are often consumed by putting out brush fire after brush fire. In this climate, it may seem more efficient to tell others what to do, dismiss them and return our focus to the crisis du jour. Don't fall into this trap.

Listening communicates that you value your team members and their opinions. Make sure you are fully focused when you listen to others. Stop what you are doing and engage. Maintain eye contact with the speaker. Watch for nonverbal cues and body language so you can fully interpret what the person is trying to say.

I was recently coaching an executive who wanted to take our conversation in a specific direction. In coaching, we want the client to set the agenda for the conversation. This was my second session with this particular client, so I didn't know her very well. Within the first 15 minutes, I sensed tension in her. I said I felt like she was dealing with a great amount of stress. The "tough as nails" executive became emotional and quickly acknowledged that stress was consuming her life. She was overloaded at work, feeling taken advantage of by colleagues and unable to dedicate enough time to her family. By the end of our time together, I suggested that the stress in her life was an urgent situation that she needed to make a priority. We shifted our next several coaching sessions to helping her develop strategies to manage stress and eliminate the negative energy the pressure was causing in her. Active listening involves paying attention to what is not being said as well as the actual words that are being spoken.

## #2: Mentor and coach them.

Some of the most rewarding experiences I have had in my career have involved mentoring reporters and anchors when I worked in the television news business. I loved it when a reporter would bring a sample of their work into my office and we would watch stories he or she had produced. Though I always felt like I was getting more out of the sessions than they were, I most enjoyed the look on their faces when they would leave my office. I could tell that those team members greatly valued my decision to invest some of myself into them. In fact, I believe that people value those opportunities even more than a raise.

Of course, mentoring and coaching requires a significant time commitment—but your investment of time will pay off in spades for everyone involved. One of the biggest frustrations I've experienced in mentoring is the number of times sessions are cancelled due the press of everyday business. Once you commit to mentoring/coaching in your culture, stand firm in that commitment and be realistic about what that commitment involves for all parties. Take a sensible approach that involves learning to walk before you run. The increase in employee engagement and retention will make your commitment to mentoring and coaching worth your while.

## #3: Affirm them.

When you affirm your team members and let them know you believe in them, you inspire, encourage and motivate them. Let them know you are on their side and are willing to go the extra mile to help THEM achieve THEIR dreams. Let them know that what is important to THEM is important to YOU and give them a chance to try new things. Lastly, inspire and motivate them to achieve goals that they didn't even think were possible.

## #4: Challenge them.

We are capable of doing much more than we think we can do. Often it takes a leader who can see that potential to coax it out of us. We need to be challenged to take action that we might otherwise shy away from.

When I managed a television newsroom, at the beginning of each day we would determine what stories we would cover and assign crews to produce each story. One particular morning, we had sent everyone off on their assignments when a piece of breaking news changed the day dramatically. This breaking story would be what we called the "lead" or the first story in the newscast. The lead story is usually assigned to one of our best veteran reporters.

In order to designate a veteran reporter to the new lead for the day, we would have to make several shifts in our coverage assignments, which was not unusual in that business. The only other option would be to assign the story to a rookie reporter who was working her very first day on the job. That was simply unheard of in the newsroom. Rookies, even very good ones, usually have to prove themselves over several weeks before they earn such a prestigious assignment.

Even so, I decided to go with the rookie. I surrounded her with the best resources we had to support her. I assigned our senior videographer to shoot the story, introduce her to news sources on the scene and coached her on questions to ask and how to edit the story. Several other team members helped with writing and other production logistics.

Though she didn't want to admit it to me, the rookie was scared to death. I'm sure she was thinking, "What have I gotten myself into?" In the end, with the support of her colleagues, the story ended up being very good—most worthy of the lead story in the newscast. It was interesting to watch her body language during the day. As she left the newsroom at the end of the day, I could see the transition from scared rookie to a reporter with great self-confidence. Her body language seemed to say, "Yeah, I've got this!"

I don't know how much challenging her that day contributed to her development as a professional. However, I do know that she has gone on to a very successful career in the industry, which has spanned more than three decades.

## #5: Hold them accountable.

It is easy to understand why so many leaders (myself included), struggle with holding people accountable. We as humans tend to shy away from difficult, uncomfortable conversations.

In his best-selling book, *The Five Dysfunctions of a Team* (Jossey-Bass 2002), author Patrick Lencioni says holding people accountable is "an act of love." According to Lencioni, when you withhold feedback from someone, you are not giving them a chance to improve, which is the "worst disservice you can do for them." (3)

When I work in a one-on-one coaching relationship, I close each session by asking my client to commit to taking a manageable step towards achieving one of their goals before our next coaching session. That little piece of homework is a way to build progress and accountability into the coaching relationship. The clients know they have to answer to the coach as to whether they fulfilled their commitment. By holding people accountable, we are helping them make concrete progress in their career and developing discipline and consistency in their work.

## COACHING TIPS

**Coaching Tip #1:** Take a few minutes today to reflect on the person or people who made a difference in your career because they believed in your potential. What impact have they had on your career?

**Coaching Tip #2:** Start each day by asking yourself this question: How can I add value into the life of one person in my world today?

# LEADERSHIP INSIGHT #3:

# Celebrate the Small Milestones

*"Take advantage of each small success. In this way you
close the gap between what you want from life and what
it is giving you."—Deepak Chopra*

The first few months of Sharen's recovery were filled with uncertainty, doubt and excruciatingly slow progress. Based on the initial medical prognosis, we had no idea if she would talk, walk or even be able to sit up on her own again. During this time, any positive signs would be cause for celebration.

The speech therapist at the hospital suggested that we have some fun with Sharen and sing songs to encourage her to speak. About three days after her stroke, our son (who has always had a playful relationship with his mom) led the first breakthrough as he was joking with Sharen. Suddenly, she responded to the fun by saying, "Hi." I never imagined that a simple two-letter salutation could bring such joy into our lives. A few days later, we were singing Happy Birthday to our daughter, and suddenly Sharen joined in the singing. In the midst of this deep valley in our lives, we experienced hope that lifted our spirits and filled our hearts.

After nine days in the hospital, Sharen was discharged to the rehab center where she spent six and a half weeks. Her progress remained slow despite almost daily physical, occupational and speech therapy. It wasn't until a couple of days before she was discharged (another insurance mandate) that she could stand up with assistance. The thought of her walking again seemed like a fantasy.

For the next four months, Sharen had home therapy eight times a week. After a few weeks, she was able to take steps using a walker—a huge breakthrough. The stroke compromised the right side of her body, so as a right-handed person, she had to learn to write with her left hand. Her speech came along slowly as she found it difficult to put her thoughts into words. She often commented that she felt "discombobulated."

After she completed home therapy, Sharen continued six months of out-patient physical therapy. By the time she completed this therapy, she was able to walk with a walker, but she could not negotiate steps. This gave her the ability to at least enjoy trips to public places, including stores, restaurants, church, etc. Her speech continued to improve especially as she grew more confident in her abilities to communicate.

Though Sharen will never regain all the independence she had before the stroke, she is able to walk, talk and enjoy what is most important in her life: the love of her family and friends. Today, she successfully manages her role as a homemaker with very little assistance from me and, thankfully, continues to serve as our household's chief executive officer and primary decision maker!

The "tiny" victories that we have celebrated along the way offered us hope, encouragement and confidence that Sharen would continue to gain strength and overcome many of the challenges she faced during her recovery. To this day, we continue to celebrate each milestone. So often in life, we focus on the big dreams and goals we seek to attain—and that is a good thing. However, if we're always focused on the big picture, we can lose sight of the importance of smaller accomplishments that pave the way to the larger breakthroughs in life. We need to take time to appreciate the value of smaller milestones in our careers and lives.

## BE INTENTIONAL ABOUT CELEBRATING SMALL MILESTONES

In leadership, the busyness of the day can cause us to lose sight of those smaller milestones. For many leaders, celebrating the smaller stuff isn't something that they find particularly important—after all, those accomplishments are simply expected. Yet, for your team, smaller milestones can be incredibly important. This is particularly true if you are navigating a change, which is pretty much constant in this day. While many team members are slow to embrace change, they are more likely to get on board once they experience progress. Taking time to celebrate the small victories will solidify their support, bolster their confidence and motivate them to charge ahead towards the larger goal.

In their groundbreaking book entitled *The Progress Principle, Using Small Wins to Ignite Joy, Engagement and Creativity at Work* (Harvard Business Review Press 2011), authors Teresa Amabile and Steven Kramer detail the impact of small steps in progress. (1) Over the course of several years, the two researchers studied seven companies in depth, including 12,000 employee diary entries. The data they collected showed that progress at work feeds what the authors label "inner work life," which involves your emotions, perceptions and motivation. The authors concluded that facilitating progress is the most effective way for leaders to make a positive impact on inner work life—which directly affects productivity.

> *"Even when progress happens in small steps, a person's sense of steady forward movement toward an important goal can make all the difference between a great day and a terrible one…People's inner work lives seemed to lift or drag depending on whether or not their projects moved forward, even by small increments. Small wins often had a surprisingly strong positive effect." (2)—Teresa Amabile and Steven Kramer*

This reminds me of when I was coaching an IT manager for a large insurance company. His work life was a constant barrage of e-mails from team members asking him to assist with their IT needs. Fighting exhaustion, the harried IT manager had established improved work life balance as his number one goal for the coaching program. I urged him to find a way to regularly disconnect from his phone so he could break free of the constant stress caused by his colleagues' e-mail demands. My coachee insisted there was no way he could unplug from the technology because of the frustrations it would cause among co-workers unable to reach him for a few hours.

In a follow-up coaching session, the IT manager told me his wife encouraged him to unplug in the evenings, which he agreed to do. (I had to get over the blow to my ego that he didn't accept his coach's suggestion to do the same. I applauded him for doing the right thing and, more importantly, for being a good husband!) The IT manager noticed instant results. He started to feel more relaxed and sleep better. To his absolute amazement, the world at work didn't fall apart because he disconnected himself from his e-mail. The insurance company continued to operate just fine without him for a few hours! After enjoying his initial success at unplugging in the evenings, the IT Manager came to the next coaching session and announced he also was going to start unplugging on the weekends. The initial small step he took to unplug during evenings had given him the confidence and motivation to take a bigger step towards achieving the work life balance he had been craving. Amabile and Kramer noted similar results in their research:

> *"Progress motivates people to accept difficult challenges more readily and to persist longer. If people feel capable, then they see difficult problems as positive challenges and opportunities to succeed. Put another way, they develop a 'sense of empowerment.'" (3)*—*Teresa Amabile and Steven Kramer*

## THE BENEFITS OF CELEBRATIONS

Former football coach and pastor Tom Mullins talks about how he learned of the importance of celebration in his career and life. He points out five benefits of celebration (4):

### #1: Celebration demonstrates you value your team.

One of the draining realities of the television business was the constant emphasis on winning the ratings battle. Viewer ratings determine advertising rates and, consequently, the fate of many careers. Whenever our team won an important ratings contest, we made sure to throw a celebratory pizza party. TV was always a "what have you done for me lately" business, so we used the momentum we generated from our temporary victory and pizza celebration to spur us on to the next ratings challenge.

> *"Celebrating your people demonstrates that you value them and you acknowledge their part in making the victory possible. Simply put, your people need to feel valued and affirmed by their leader." (5)—Tom Mullins*

## #2: Celebration reinforces core organizational values. (6)

If you are intentional about affirming the contributions of your team members, you are "walking the walk" when it comes to living out your organizational values. Your values are the foundation of the culture that you build and maintain. Celebrating success underscores your commitment to those values and communicates to the team that "this is who we are."

## #3: Celebration builds team morale. (7)

This is particularly true when you are in the midst of a challenging project or implementing a difficult change. When you recognize progress, this builds confidence among team members. Taking a pause to celebrate a milestone lifts spirits in amazing ways. It will bond the team in a unifying spirit and encourage them to view the next mountain they climb as less daunting.

## #4: Celebration increase retention and productivity.

Mullins cites data that shows that a large number of people leave their jobs because they feel unappreciated. (8) It also has been well documented that most people quit their boss, not the organization. Retaining great talent isn't about money. People want to feel appreciated and be recognized for their work. Celebrating progress not only meets those needs, it also results in higher levels of engagement and productivity.

### #5: Celebration is a great recruiting tool. (9)

When you build a work culture that celebrates progress and affirms and recognizes the contributions of team members, job candidates know about it. When potential employees are considering where they want to work, they pay close attention to the culture. A culture that lives its values, loves its people and celebrates small milestones will rise to the top of the most desired places to work list.

## HOW TO CELEBRATE SMALL MILESTONES WITH YOUR TEAM

There really is no limit to the ways you can celebrate milestone moments. These celebrations can be as small as a simple "thank you," or they could be larger events, parties and activities. It matters not so much <u>what</u> you do but more so that you take time to pause and let your team savor the moment.

Also, it is important to recognize that people are different and not everyone wants to celebrate in the same way. I remember one manager who told me he was trying to organize team bonding activities, such as bowling. He was repeatedly frustrated by two employees who didn't like leaving the office for activities like that. Obviously, they did not like bowling and other out-of-the-office activities, so I suggested that the manager ask them what they would prefer instead.

Have a discussion with your team about the activities they enjoy. Here's a handful of suggestions for celebrating milestone moments:

**Serve cake and a toast.** Bring in a cake and give a quick toast (non-alcoholic is fine). This is a nice touch for celebrating when new employees have a specific breakthrough.

**Publish a blog, email or video.** Celebrating a team success by sharing it with the world is a nice touch. This is something team members may want to share with family, friends and others. However, be careful about taking this approach for individual accomplishments. Some folks don't like public recognition and prefer a quiet pat on the back for a job well done.

**Do something fun.** Take the team out to lunch or plan a fun bonding activity like kayaking or a cooking or painting class. Go to a ballgame, an archery range or visit a museum. It can do a world of good for folks just to get away from the office for a while.

**Give them a day off.** It could even be a half day—Friday afternoons are always a favorite. This is a great reward when the workload has been constant and people are starting to wear down. Simply celebrating the fact that your team made it through a tough stretch will be appreciated.

**Offer a cash bonus.** Everyone appreciates a few extra bucks, but be careful with this one. People can come to expect bonuses, and they may be disappointed when they don't receive one. This actually can become a demotivator. Gift cards are also a nice occasional bonus.

**Share the high spots.** Take a few minutes every week to have folks share their big win. This can be done at the start of a regular team meeting or as a separate activity. I worked with one team that included this as a high-low activity, where team members shared a big win and also their biggest disappointment for the week. This improved communications, helped folks get to know each other better and provided regular opportunities for celebrating milestones.

**Ring the bell.** Some sales departments have a bell that account executives ring when they make their budget or a big sale. Other departments have a win-sharing board. These also can be used for smaller milestones, such as finally securing an appointment with a potential client who has been difficult to reach.

There is no right way or wrong way to celebrate small milestones. Do what works for your team, the unique situation and the budget. Acknowledging and celebrating small milestones is easy and fun. When you make this a regular practice, it will lead to bigger victories and even more celebrations down the road.

## COACHING TIPS

**Coaching Tip #1:** What is your next big project or change initiative? Identify small milestones that can be celebrated along the way.

**Coaching Tip #2:** Write down annual goals and review them quarterly. Celebrate every small step in progress.

## LEADERSHIP INSIGHT #4:

# Discover the Power of Positivity

*"Being positive won't guarantee you'll succeed but being negative will guarantee you won't."*
*—Jon Gordon*

The journey Sharen has endured since her stroke has been filled with a seemingly never-ending series of challenges that I am convinced would have crushed many people. In addition to the grueling months of therapy and years of tests and medical appointments (how many doctors can one person have?), she fought a battle with cancer that included nine months of chemo and radiation therapy. She also had a shoulder replacement, which meant six weeks before she could be cleared for weight-bearing on the new shoulder. This meant no walking during that time as she needed the weight bearing to use her walker—that was a real challenge!

As difficult as the physical challenges were, Sharen was equally impacted by the loss of contact with many friends. Sharen has always been a very relational person, so it was difficult for her to accept that many people, including some of her best friends, would stop calling as they moved on with their lives while she adjusted to her new reality. The old adage "out-of-sight, out-of-mind" never seemed so real and so painful.

One of Sharen's greatest attributes—and she has many—is that she has always been one of the most positive human beings you'll ever meet. She wakes up with a cheerful disposition, even before her morning cup of coffee! She greets others with a smile and is quick to make friends wherever she goes. There is no question that her positivity was a major contributor to her recovery and the quality of life she enjoys today. Sharen <u>believed</u> she would walk again. She willed herself to be a high-functioning human being who could enjoy life despite the numerous barriers she confronts every day. While she understandably has a few bad moments along the way, she never stays down for long. If there is such a thing as a bounce-back factor, hers would be among the highest scores around.

## POSITIVITY OVERCOMES NEGATIVITY

Your ability to remain positive in the face of the daily challenges you face as a leader has a huge impact on your success. One of the biggest hurdles leaders must overcome is battling relentless negativity that is often so pervasive in the workplace. Negativity is contagious. It is easy for others to fall prey to negative attitudes, which are destructive to team productivity and engagement. As a leader you must rise above the negativity and model the behavior you want to develop in others. Being positive doesn't mean that you wear rose-colored glasses, resist tackling thorny problems and overlook downward trends. It simply means that no matter the challenge you and the team face, you will remain positive about your ability to overcome those challenges.

The good news is that positivity is equally as contagious as negativity. It requires leaders who insist on going there and coach and mentor their team members to do the same. Others will notice your positive approach. Most people will admire your positivity and begin to adopt many of the same behaviors. A positive approach will organically grow in your organization and has the ability to radically transform your culture.

In *The Power of Positive Leadership* (John Wiley & Sons, Inc. 2017), author Jon Gordon writes that in leadership your positivity must be greater than all the negativity.

> *"Be more positive than the negativity you face. Don't be afraid of it. Negativity is like a barking dog. It seems powerful, but when you look it in the eyes, it runs away."*
> *(1)—Jon Gordon*

Gordon says the first step in removing negativity in the workplace is to transform the culture. You can do this by insisting that negativity won't be tolerated, implement a no complaining rule, listen to critical comments with empathy and love, and, when necessary, get rid of people who refuse to stop being negative.

I often hear people say they can't transform a negative culture because they do not have the positional authority to make changes. My response is that leadership is not a position on an organizational chart. No matter what our position is, we can and should role model positive behavior, which will make a difference in influencing the behavior of others. Jon Gordon writes that you should "lead from where you are."

He says, "Become a positive energy that demonstrates to others what real positivity in the form of love, patience, kindness and care looks like." (2)

## NEGATIVE VOICES ARE ALL AROUND US

Leaders in civil rights and freedom movements around the world have had to fight through solidly entrenched barriers, many of which have been in place for centuries. Martin Luther King Jr. led a struggle to end racism in America—a drive that faced bitter resistance and negativity in virtually every community where he visited, marched and spoke. His powerful, positive and inspirational messages encouraged millions to join the American civil rights movement. His vision and legacy are most remembered in his stirring "I Have a Dream" speech, which instilled hope and determination in followers around the globe—many of whom continue to work tirelessly to see his vision become a reality.

Mahatma Gandhi is another example of a transformational leader who overcame huge odds to provide people with a positive sense of direction and purpose. He was able to convert a fragmented freedom drive into a true mass movement. By preaching his theory of civil disobedience, not only was Gandhi able to bring all citizens of India into the freedom struggle, but his platform of non-violence became the model for civil rights and freedom struggles around the world.

As a leader, you will hear voices of negativity that form resistance to every new idea, every change and every innovation you advance. Those voices can and should be useful in helping you strengthen your ideas, identify and overcome barriers and eventually win over stakeholders who are slow to warm to your proposals. However, negative forces are often so powerful that leaders become afraid to move forward. Those voices of resistance can hammer away at your confidence and paralyze your organization. In the meantime, your competitors will forge ahead while your team remains locked in the status quo.

## INTERNAL VOICES CAN BE MOST DAMAGING

In addition to the voices of negativity that surround us, we often fall victim to the negative voices from within. Rick Carson gives a name to these destructive voices that many of us hear. In his book, *Taming Your Gremlin* (HarperCollins Publishers 2009), Carson says the gremlin is the source of your negative thoughts.

> *"He is with you when you wake up in the morning and when you go to sleep at night. He tells you who and how you are, and he defines and interprets your every experience. He wants you to accept his interpretations as reality, and his goal, from moment to moment, day to day, is to squelch the natural, vibrant you within."*
> *(3)—Rick Carson*

Carson says the first step in overcoming those negative voices is to be aware of them. It is important to maintain the perspective that internal voices are normal—everyone hears them, not just you.

"As you begin to simply notice your gremlin, you will become acutely sensitive to the fact that you are not your gremlin, but rather his observer. You will see clearly that your gremlin has no real hold on you. As this awareness develops, you will begin to appreciate and enjoy your life more and more," Carson writes. (4)

Believe it or not, these negative voices can prove useful in reshaping our ideas and approach. The key is for you to control the voices and not the other way around. Some days it is most effective to say "enough is enough," and simply choose to ignore the voices, knowing that the direction you have chosen is the right way to go.

As a leader, positivity will help you overcome barriers and conquer mountains that seem insurmountable to others. An authentic, positive attitude is not only contagious, but it also inspires those around you. By demonstrating positivity, you will instill in your team a drive to achieve goals that, in many cases, they never dreamed possible.

## POSITIVE LEADERSHIP DRIVES POSITIVE ORGANIZATIONAL RESULTS

Your positivity as a leader sets the tone for a positive culture, which in turn will lead to better results in key metrics. Kim Cameron, professor at the Ross School of Business at the University of Michigan, has studied the effects of positive leadership. His research shows a link between positive leadership and an increase in job satisfaction, well-being, engagement and performance. The energy created by positive leadership also has been shown to improve team cohesion, experimentation and innovation. (5) In a recent meta-analysis study, it was shown that focusing on the positive has a significant impact on work productivity, brain activity, social relationships and physical and mental health. (6)

There also has been considerable research around positive-to-negative ratios (PNR), which quantifies the number of positive versus negative interactions. Psychologist John Gottman has conducted extensive research involving PNR ratios in marriage. Using a 5:1 ratio as "the magic ratio," Gottman's team predicted whether 700 newlywed couples would stay together or divorce by scoring their positive and negative interactions in a single 15-minute conversation. Ten years later, the follow-up showed they predicted divorce with 94 percent accuracy. (7) Similarly, psychologist Barbara Fredrickson and mathematician Marcial Losada found that work teams with a PNR greater than 3:1 were significantly more productive than work teams with a lower ratio. (8)

When you maintain a positive outlook as a leader, you have the power to drive change and impact positive outcomes in numerous areas. Of that, I am positive!

## MAINTAINING A POSITIVE CULTURE

As a leader, you are driving the bus when it comes to modeling positive behavior and its impact on those around you and the culture. Here are a few other things you will want to hard-wire as part of your positive leadership DNA:

**Communicate positive messages.** Be conscious of your word choice. Think emotional intelligence. Don't gloss over setbacks or minimize challenges, but identify the silver lining and opportunities that are available as a result of those difficulties. Be the leader who sees the path forward and lead your team down that path.

**Hire positive people.** There are some signals to look for during those all-important interviews. Pay attention to body language. Ask them about challenges they have faced in life and how they dealt with them. Give them a scenario that could occur at work and ask how they would handle it. What do they say about past employers? Look into assessments that can help you determine their positivity factor.

**Emphasize positive relationships.** Promote positive problem solving within your team. Help your employees recognize the common ground. Embrace diversity in thinking and encourage all points of view. Celebrate the differences in people and promote the appreciation of the unique contributions of all team members.

**Shut down negative behavior.** There is a big difference between constructive suggestions and chronic negativity. It's critical to discuss legitimate concerns and hold each other accountable. However, complaining for the sake of complaining or living a life where the glass is always half empty is draining and counterproductive. Root out gossip, bad attitudes and disrespectful behavior. Shift conversations into more productive directions.

**Encourage work-life balance.** All team members will be their best when they are able to enjoy life to the fullest outside of work. With that said, it can be difficult for many dedicated team members to shut down their work life and unplug from technology on the weekends. As a leader, you should insist on this. Create a culture where people are assigned to cover for employees who are out sick or on vacation. Get your folks out of the office. Insist they take their personal days and vacation time. Work-life balance not only makes employees happier and more productive, but it also is a key factor in attracting and retaining talent.

**Smile.** It may seem simple, but nothing promotes positivity like a smile. Smiling relaxes you and those around you. Like positivity, a smile is contagious. God gave you that smile to share. Take full advantage.

Positivity boosts employee wellness. Positivity empowers you as a leader and inspires the team. It creates a culture that not only produces great results, but one that talented people will seek out because they know they will flourish in that environment.

## COACHING TIPS

**Coaching Tip #1:** During a team meeting, break employees into pairs. Ask each person to offer one positive characteristic their partner brings to the team. End the exercise with a large group debrief.

**Coaching Tip #2:** Ask yourself and your team, what are the voices you hear? What are your strategies for overcoming those voices?

# LEADERSHIP INSIGHT #5:

# Maintain an Attitude of Gratitude

*"So much has been given to me; I have no time to ponder over that which has been denied."—Helen Keller*

Considering the initial prognosis we received when Sharen entered the hospital and the agonizing uncertainty surrounding her recovery, the quality of life she enjoys today is cause for daily celebration in our family. As I reflect back on those first few hours, days, weeks and months, I now realize that I used to take the simple things in life for granted—such as being able to form a thought, speak, walk, perform mundane tasks, dress, shower and simply enjoy the presence of people I love.

I am so incredibly grateful for the support we have received in the years since Sharen suffered her stroke. I am grateful for a job that provided good health insurance, the love of our family and friends, our church, and so many people lifting us up in prayer. I am grateful for Sharen's contagious enthusiasm, her smile and her dogged determination to overcome the daily challenges she faces. For someone who hates grocery shopping, I have come to treasure our weekly trips to the store, which have become an important outing Sharen and I take together.

Though she can walk short distances, Sharen is unable to navigate steps, which makes it pretty much impossible to visit friends in their homes. Travel, in general, is difficult. We are blessed to have a lovely deck that sits on a wooded lot in the rear of our home. That has become our weekend cottage—our getaway. I appreciate the simplicity and the beauty that sits right outside our back door.

What Sharen misses the most is the ability to drive. She must depend on others to take her places. Rather than allowing this frustration to consume her, she instead chooses to treasure the daily moments—whether it's enjoying a phone call from a friend or a Facetime session with our daughter and her two puppies, whose antics entertain Sharen no end.

We can't control many of the circumstances we face in life. We can control how we choose to relate to those circumstances. It is easy, and I would argue understandable, to allow our circumstances to make us bitter, dejected and resentful. It is often assumed that happiness is a direct result of our circumstances. Yet, contemporary research tells us it is the other way around. Happiness is, in fact, a choice. When we choose to appreciate what we have rather than be consumed by what we don't have, we will experience true happiness in life.

Maintaining an attitude of gratitude will also have a major impact on your work as a leader. Of course, leaders must deal with daily frustrations: worrying about personnel challenges, making sales quotas, competitive threats, legal and regulatory requirements and constant demands on our time. Technology has us plugged into the world 24/7, and we are often overworked, overloaded with commitments and stressed out to the max. Something always needs to be fixed in our world, and we take on the burden of fixing it. As leaders, we are often consumed with all of the things that are broken. However, what we really need to program into our lives is the ability to unplug, step back and be grateful for all the things in life that *aren't* broken.

As leaders, how many times have we overlooked the steady excellence of people around us who get the job done every day without fanfare or drama? How often do we forget to say "thank you" for a job well done? How often do we take for granted the jobs we have, the communities where we live and the everyday relationships that add richness to our existence and contribute so much to our success?

## IS THE GLASS HALF-EMPTY OR HALF-FULL?

The first radio station where I worked was tiny and operated on a very small budget. Our equipment was old and not always functioning at what I would call broadcast quality standards. Being a proud professional who cared about the quality of our broadcast product, I often found that my frustrations with the equipment were negatively impacting my attitude. Many years later as I look back on that time in my life, I realize how fortunate I was to have a job in a business I loved dearly and such great passion for the work I performed each day. Though it was appropriate to feel some frustrations, I was wrong to allow it to affect my attitude in the workplace.

My second radio job was with a much larger station in Lansing, Michigan. Compared to my previous station, the equipment was top-notch—I thought I had died and gone to heaven! After a few weeks working there, I noticed everyone else complained about the poor equipment. I couldn't believe it. I remember thinking, "What's wrong with you people? You don't appreciate how good you have it."

The same scenario played out every place I worked. I noticed a recurring cycle: people would complain and they would be miserable.

If the owners bought new equipment or technology, the employees would soon begin to grumble about something else. We (myself often included) rarely seemed to appreciate what we had.

As I look back on those experiences, I understand how feeling gratitude is a choice we make in life. Gratitude is not only beneficial for our emotional well-being; it also can make a difference in how we feel physically. Gratitude is contagious.

## THE SCIENCE ON GRATITUDE

As leaders, most of us instinctively buy in to the notion that we should regularly practice and demonstrate gratitude. There is plenty of research that shows gratitude may be one of the most powerful tools we have to motivate, encourage and empower our teams. Gratitude also is essential when it comes to building better, stronger relationships throughout the organization.

Dr. Robert Emmons and Dr. Michael E. McCullough have conducted extensive research on gratitude. In one study, the researchers asked participants to write a few sentences each week. The first group wrote about what made them feel grateful, the second group wrote about daily irritations and the third group wrote about events that had affected them. After 10 weeks, the group who wrote about their gratitude were more optimistic and felt better about their lives. (1)

Martin Seligman tested the impact of positive psychology interventions on 411 people. When participants were asked to write and deliver a letter of gratitude to someone they had never thanked for their role in their lives, their happiness scores soared. Yet another example: Researchers at Wharton School at the University of Pennsylvania randomly divided university fundraisers into two groups.

The first group made fundraising calls as they had always done. The second group first received an encouraging talk from a manager who told the team how grateful she was for their efforts. During the next week, the university fundraisers who heard the message of gratitude made 50 percent more calls than the other group. (2)

The results of these studies seem perfectly clear: People work harder and produce better results for managers who show gratitude for their efforts. There is also a direct connection between gratitude and a person's well-being, which manifests itself in all parts of their life, especially work.

## THE STORY OF MY CHRISTMAS TIE

The topic of gratitude always makes me think about a former coworker at the television station where I worked. Mike joined the station as an intern in our production department. Although challenged with a disability, he was very capable of performing tasks assigned to him by our production manager. After Mike served as an intern for several months, a paid, part-time job became available. It involved operating a studio camera during our morning newscasts. Our production manager recommended to me that we hire Mike for the job, which he had earned based on his work as an intern. I agreed, and Mike happily accepted.

The part-time positions in our production department were low-paying jobs and usually involved less than desirable work hours—often very early in the morning, late evenings, weekends and holidays. The jobs typically were held by college students hoping to use the part-time work as a foothold to break into the business. Thanks to the combination of low pay and crummy hours, many of these part-time employees did not enjoy their jobs. Mike was different. He had the most positive attitude I have ever seen in a human being. He LOVED that job!

To express his appreciation, Mike gave me a Christmas tie. That was more than 20 years ago, and I still wear that tie every Christmas season. When I am complimented on the tie, which happens often, I take the opportunity to share the story about Mike. It is a story of how he refused to allow challenging circumstances in his life to defeat him. It is a story of how he viewed a job considered undesirable by others as something of great value and meaning in his life. Mike went on to earn a bachelor's degree and now works for an organization that provides employment opportunities for people with disabilities. A few years ago, he was named employee of the year. Mike is admired by all who know him. By any definition of success, at work or at home, he is a shining example of how an attitude of gratitude can make a huge difference in our outlook, happiness, productivity and relationships with others.

## EXPRESSING GRATITUDE

Life was crashing down on John Kralik in a major way. His business as an attorney was failing. He had no money to offer his staff year-end bonuses. His office landlord had cancelled his lease, and he had no money for another office. He was divorced, paying a mortgage on three households and his girlfriend had dumped him right before Christmas. One of his children was regularly borrowing money, which he said seemed more like cash infusions. He was overweight and overworked.

One day in the midst of his depression, Kralik went for a long walk in the woods near his home in Pasadena, California. A voice kept telling him he was a loser. Then another voice broke through—from where, he does not know. The voice said:

*"Until you learn to be grateful for the things you have, you will not receive the things you want."—John Kralik (3)*

After that, Kralik decided to thank someone every day for the next year. He wrote 365 thank you notes to 365 different individuals. It wasn't always easy—especially at first, as he struggled to think of who to thank. Eventually, several things became apparent to him. Above all else, he found that the regular act of showing appreciation impacted his attitude. When people asked how he was, he stopped talking about his numerous problems and instead shared things for which he was grateful. Over time, others around him began to do the same thing. In his wonderful book, *A Simple Act of Gratitude: How Learning to Say Thank You Changed My Life* (Hachette Books 2010), Kralik discusses how writing thank you notes transformed his life. (4)

## APPRECIATE WHAT OTHERS BRING TO YOUR TEAM

Leaders often find themselves trapped in what I like to call the "fix-it" mindset. That's because day in and day out, they find themselves putting out fires. Life seems to be an endless effort of rushing from one brush fire to another. We have to fix what is broken and, when there is time, we must figure out why the project or process got off track. In this chaotic organizational lifestyle, "fixing" brokenness usually means focusing on what people do wrong—and ultimately our attention is drawn to weaknesses in others.

Of course, we should not ignore the need to fix things, and as leaders it's important to help others identify and strengthen weaknesses. However, I would argue that leaders and their organizations will get much farther ahead by intentionally focusing on and appreciating the good things our team members bring to the organization each day. By showing appreciation for those positive characteristics, we motivate our team members and encourage them to continue to bring those attributes to the forefront.

When it comes to building a culture of appreciation, one of the most effective tools I have found is CliftonStrengths™ from Gallup. Known as the Father of Strengths-Based Psychology, Donald Clifton created the CliftonStrengths assessment, which identifies 34 themes or strengths. When you take the CliftonStrengths assessment (formerly Clifton StrengthsFinder), you will learn your top five strengths. I highly recommend this assessment for you and your team, which can be accessed by visiting www.gallup.com/cliftonstrengths or purchasing the book *StrengthFinder 2.0* (Gallup Press 2007) by Tom Rath. (5)

As a leader, there are wonderful coaching opportunities available to you when you know the strengths of each of your team members. First, you will help others identify and appreciate characteristics that, in some cases, they not even view as a personal strength. You also can develop strategies to help employees bring their strengths to the forefront more regularly, which benefits the entire team. You can begin to build that culture where each team member recognizes and embraces others for the unique strengths they bring to the table.

Gallup has conducted decades worth of research that lends strong support to using a strengths-based approach to leadership. Research has shown that teams using a strengths-based approach are more productive, often more profitable and have employees with higher levels of engagement and tend to stay with the organization longer. (6) It makes sense when you think about it. After all, this approach allows people to spend more time performing activities they are passionate about.

## YOU REAP WHAT YOU SOW

It has clearly been shown that the regular, authentic use of gratitude is a powerful advantage to your team. When you maintain an attitude of gratitude, it also will benefit you as a leader and a human being in countless ways. Here are just a few of the benefits you'll enjoy:

### #1: You'll gain their respect and trust.

Genuine gratitude is a virtue that people admire and appreciate. People will respect your authenticity. You'll also build a foundation of trust on which all great things in an organization are built.

### #2: Improved professional skills.

According to research, gratitude improves decision-making and increases goal achievement and productivity.

### #3: You'll boost your PNR ratio.

In the previous chapter on positivity, I wrote about research regarding the number of positive interactions relative to the number of negative interactions. That is known as your PNR ratio—and this ratio is increased through the regular practice of displaying gratitude.

## #4: Improved emotional health.

Gratitude has been linked to more happiness, less depression and enhancements in self-esteem and resilience.

## #5: Improved physical health.

People who consistently demonstrate gratitude report feeling better, sleeping better, having less pain and lower blood pressure and feeling less stressed. Try it. It works!

Show gratitude. Appreciating others will not only transform you as an individual and a leader, it also will transform your organization. All it takes is a simple thank you or recognition of a job well done. By acknowledging and bringing the strengths of team members to the forefront, you'll create an engaging environment where employees will want to stay for the long haul. Even better? It's also good for the bottom line!

### COACHING TIPS

**Coaching Tip #1:** Create a list of things for which you are grateful. Write a thank you note for each one.

**Coaching Tip #2:** Conduct a team-building exercise where every team member expresses one characteristic they appreciate about each member of the team.

# LEADERSHIP INSIGHT #6:

# Humility is the Ultimate Strength

*"Humility is not thinking less of yourself. It is thinking of yourself less."—Ken Blanchard*

One of Sharen's greatest attributes is the love she has for others. She has demonstrated this love every day of her life by always putting others first, especially her family. I suppose that earlier in my life I didn't spend too much time reflecting on this because I was busy enjoying being the beneficiary of her love and attention. Put another way, the more unselfish Sharen was, the more selfish I became.

Sharen always put our needs first. In the process of doing so, she often denied herself of things—whether it was clothes, other physical possessions or simply the use of her time. Her priority in life was taking care of others. She was always the friend who listened to everyone's problems, rarely sharing her own.

Sharen's attitude of humble service towards those she loves had a most unfortunate downside. She didn't do the best job of taking care of herself. For a variety of reasons, mostly due to unfortunate experiences with medical professionals, she hated going to the doctor. Eventually, her neglect of her own health caught up with her, and she suffered a severe stroke that almost cost her life.

Since her stroke, Sharen likes to joke that turnabout is fair play. She says she spent her life taking care of me and now it is my turn to take care of her. The experience has opened my eyes to many realizations—particularly how Sharen's humility has played into who she is as a person and as the glue that holds our family together.

As her caregiver, I've realized that I must put her needs ahead of mine. Through the years, I have gotten much better at this, which I think proves the notion that humility can be learned. I confess there are many days when I do not do the best job of putting her first. I will never be in the same league as Sharen when it comes to humility. To use a baseball analogy, she is a major league all-star while I am languishing in the minors.

I also have realized that Sharen will never stop being the same humble person with a deep desire to serve her family. It took a while for me to understand how important it is for her to do things for me. I have learned to resist the temptation to do certain things myself in favor of letting her perform the job. She needs that and I still enjoy being the beneficiary of her humble heart!

Humility is, without question, one of the most essential attributes for successful leadership in the 21st century. Genuinely humble leaders are easier to follow, they empower others and earn the highest levels of trust. Leaders who walk the halls humbly are more relatable, inspirational and more effective in building a culture that encourages talent attraction and retention. Teams that thrive in a culture built on a foundation of humility are more productive, more profitable and serve their customers better. In his book, *Humility: The Secret Ingredient of Success* (Shiloh Run Press 2016), author Pat Williams writes:

*"Genuine humility is one of the greatest strengths a leader can possess. Humble leaders are strong enough to listen to other points of view, strong enough to admit mistakes and learn from them, strong enough to celebrate the achievements and successes of others, and strong enough to surround themselves with talented people without feeling threatened or diminished." (1)—Pat Williams*

Notice how the word "strong" is used four times in the above quote. In the traditional, top-down or hierarchal model of leadership, humility was often associated with weakness. Increasingly, humility is understood to be an admired and sought-after trait, which is why I believe humility is the ultimate strength.

Ken Blanchard learned the value of humility in leadership at a young age. When he was elected president of his seventh-grade class, he was incredibly excited. He couldn't wait to share the news with his father, a highly decorated World War II hero. Ken couldn't have been more surprised when his father responded: "Son, it is great that you have been elected president. But now that you have that position, don't ever use it as a way of getting others to do what you want. The best use of power is not to have to use it at all. People follow great leaders because they respect them, not because they have power." (2)

## HUMBLE PIE WITH A SIDE OF IN-YOUR-FACE

Early in my management career, I received a much-needed dose of humble pie. I was working as an assignment editor in a television newsroom. In that role, I was responsible for coordinating the coverage of news, including determining what stories will be covered and what teams of reporters and videographers will cover them. It is a very demanding and stressful job that requires not only a sound understanding of news, but also the skills of an air traffic controller as you must direct and coordinate multiple teams of people throughout the day.

I was hired for the position because of my established track record as a capable street reporter who had covered news in the market for a number of years. The TV newsroom I was hired to manage was filled with eager, talented and somewhat inexperienced journalists who were hungry to do a great job—but most of them had not received adequate leadership to guide them.

I combined my practiced journalistic instincts with a direct, no-nonsense leadership style, which brought an immediate shift to the news operation and resulted in a consistent quality of reporting. The team responded in a positive fashion as they witnessed an improved team product, and their individual skills began to flourish. Within a short period of time, we were firing on all cylinders. Station management noticed the positive results and gave me a lot of credit for the new direction.

Unfortunately, I went a little overboard with my directness and tough tactics. I was impatient and lacked tolerance for mistakes, and I didn't respond well to suggestions that perhaps my approach wasn't always the best one. I became too much of a "my way or the highway" leader. There is a long-established principle that says if you overuse a strength, it becomes a weakness. I could be the poster child for that one. I was so focused on myself that I failed to notice my style was wearing people out, causing resentment and division and demoralizing the team.

Finally, the team got together and "invited" me to a staff meeting where they intended to air their grievances. One by one, they went around the room and each individual expressed their feelings. That was painful! It also was exactly what I needed. In fact, in my decades-long experience as a leader, that meeting was the best thing that had ever happened to me.

I owe an enormous debt of gratitude for the courage the men and women of that team demonstrated to call me out the way they did. That meeting reshaped me as a leader and a human being. That slice of humble pie didn't taste so great while I was eating it, but the benefits I received as a result have lasted a lifetime. After I digested that humble pie, I changed my attitude and approach as a leader. Though humility hasn't always been my strong suit, that newsroom team helped me understand that as a leader, it is not about me. That day taught me how to tune into others, care about the team and empathize with their feelings, needs and opinions. The team is first!

## THE IMPORTANCE OF HUMILITY ON THE TEAM

Best-selling author and consultant Patrick Lencioni has held a long-established practice within his organization to only hire people if they possess three virtues: they must be hungry, humble and people smart. After successfully applying this practice over a couple of decades, Lencioni decided to put his principles into a book entitled *The Ideal Team Player* (Jossey-Bass 2016). The book is an excellent primer for any leader who wants to learn how to recognize those three characteristics in people, which is not always as easy as it sounds. Lencioni says that in the context of teamwork, humility is an invaluable characteristic.

*"Great team players lack excessive ego or concerns about status. They are quick to point out contributions of others and slow to seek attention of their own. They share credit, emphasize team over self, and define success collectively rather than individually. It is no great surprise, then, that humility is the single greatest and most indispensable attribute of being a team player."*
*(3)—Patrick Lencioni*

In the book, Lencioni tells a fable about a rapidly expanding construction company that needs to do quite a bit of hiring. The team is interested in bringing a particular veteran project manager on board. This individual retired from a similar company and was interested in coming back to work. Several executives interview the candidate and easily determine that he is hungry, knowledgeable and passionate. However, trying to figure out if the candidate is humble represents a real challenge for the team. He seems like a good guy, but something doesn't seem quite right. (4)

As leaders, it can be extremely difficult to understand what humility looks like. Lencioni offers a section in his book with insightful questions you can ask a candidate to measure humility. Do they take credit for success or give it to others? Do they treat all people the same? (In this particular case, the job candidate didn't know the name of the company receptionist despite numerous opportunities to have learned it.) Does a candidate use the words "I" and "me" or do they use "we" and "us"? (5)

At the end of the day, humility on your team will end up looking like the behavior you model as a leader. Humility is a trait that can be developed. You can try to fake it, but a lack of authenticity will eventually betray you. Work to develop real humility for yourself as a leader, and then build a team culture that is centered around putting others first.

## LEADERSHIP THAT MODELS HUMILITY

During his ministry, Jesus was a model of humility and made servant leadership a centerpiece of his Last Supper preaching. During his Sermon on the Mount teaching, Jesus told his followers the "meek shall inherit the earth." (6) In contemporary American culture, we tend to think of meek people as weak sissies who often get run over by stronger-willed individuals. Being meek is hardly viewed as the way to get ahead in this world. Consider, however, the original Greek translation of the word meek, which is "power under control." Now think about some of the greatest leaders you have known and consider their leadership style in that context.

Gandhi was the central figure in India's drive for independence, advocating for civil disobedience as the means towards achieving reform. His leadership became a model for civil rights and freedom movements around the world. Desmond Tutu fought the battle against apartheid, and Pope Francis washed the feet of a parishioner as one of his first acts after being named Supreme Pontiff. Gandhi, Desmond Tutu and Pope Francis all displayed power under control in demonstrating their style of humility and servant leadership.

Mother Teresa is one of the greatest examples of humble leadership in history. In her authorized biography on Mother Teresa's life, Kathryn Spink writes: "She was, I discovered, not only humble and small but also strong willed, resolute, determined and totally fearless because God was on her side... 'What Mother wants; she gets' was a truism widely accepted among those who knew her." (7).

Mother Teresa defied conventional wisdom in her approach to serving the poor. Although church officials wanted to provide living space a distance from the neighborhoods she served, she insisted on living among the poor. Her directive to her co-workers (she insisted they be called co-workers) in the Missionaries of Charity was to "serve and not be served." Her direct personal example shaped the approach of others around her. She declined offers of a regular income because she didn't want her service to become a business. She resisted all attempts to give her credit for the success of the ministry, instead choosing to give credit to God. As her ministry grew and she became more critically acclaimed, she insisted on continuing to clean floors.

Through the years, Mother Teresa's ministry encountered numerous setbacks and frustrations that demanded patience and perseverance. As she sought to expand her highly successful ministry, she was once required by church officials to wait 10 years. The daily frustrations of trying to help the most impoverished and sick human beings on earth were so immense that others questioned why she bothered, comparing her efforts to a single drop in the ocean.

She treated everyone the same, all viewed through her lens as children of God. Awards and recognitions meant nothing to her. She used occasions of accepting awards—even the Nobel Peace Prize—to talk about the poor and God. Through it all, until the day she died, she remained unchanged in her humble yet determined approach. Physically tiny, a gentle, humble spirit, and a giant in serving others. (8)

# HOW TO BE A HUMBLE LEADER

If I asked you to rate your own humility index on a scale from 1 to 10, what number would you choose? Whatever that number may be, the next question to ask yourself is this: What specific things can you do to move that number up a couple of points? Regardless of where you fall on your self-evaluated humility index, there are several characteristics you should incorporate at a higher level in your everyday work as a leader.

## #1: Listen.

When you give your undivided attention to others, you are making their agenda the top priority. Check yourself to make sure you are actively listening. Hold eye contact. Ask questions for clarification. Block out the inevitable clutter and disruptions that try to creep into your head. When you REALLY listen to others, you are letting them know, "You matter to me."

## #2: Seek first to understand.

Don't rush to judgement and assume you know other people's intentions. Whatever you think you know about what is behind their position, you are probably wrong. Take time to explore the motivations of others. Listen (there's that word again!) to their viewpoint. Assume positive intentions on the part of others. Most of us don't listen with the intent to understand others. We listen in order to reply to them. Be genuine in your intention to truly understand where others are coming from.

### #3: Be open to suggestions.

No matter how good your idea may be, it can be made better. The best way to make it better is to encourage ideas from others. The greatest teams are the ones with leaders who cultivate a culture where everyone feels free to voice their opinions on any topic, even if it opposes the leader. The more diverse opinions, the better the universe of ideas, and consequently the better the decision. If everyone feels they have been heard and their opinion is valued, the more likely they are to buy in to the direction the group is taking.

### #4: Be vulnerable.

Admit your mistakes. This is one of the best ways to build credibility as a leader. If you're willing to admit you aren't perfect, that you don't know all the answers, or perhaps need help in a certain area, your team will respect you more. Being vulnerable makes you more real to your team. Believe me, they know more about your shortcomings than you do. So, you might as well own up to them.

### #5: Tend to others' needs.

In surveys where employees are asked what is important to them about where they work, one of the top answers is this: They want leaders who care about them and the issues they face professionally and personally. That doesn't mean you have to be everyone's best friend. It simply means that people want to know you care and will support them as they navigate issues that matter most to them.

### #6: Empower them to do their job.

In one of my leadership classes, I like to ask the question, "What have bosses done to demotivate you?" Almost every time, the number one answer is micromanaging. People absolutely hate it when their manager gives them a task or project and then promptly tells them how to do that task or project. Certainly, people need guidance and ground rules. They need training. But once they are equipped to do the job, let them do it. Your team needs to know you are there to support them if they have questions or run into barriers. Otherwise, get out of the way and let them flourish.

### #7: Give credit to others.

The other thing employees hate is when the manager insists on taking credit for the team success. Not only should you want them to receive the credit, you should pour it on them yourself.

Remember, humility does not rob you of power, but it enhances your authority as a leader. True humility also requires courage and trust that stem from a leader's confidence in themselves and their abilities.

## COACHING TIPS

**Coaching Tip #1:** Practice active listening. Take notes. Did you stop what you were doing and focus on the other person? Ask questions for clarification.

**Coaching Tip #2:** Who are the best leaders you have ever worked with? How did they demonstrate humility?

# LEADERSHIP INSIGHT #7:

# Empathy - Walk a Mile in Their Shoes

*"Empathy is the ability to step outside your own bubble*
*and into the bubbles of other people."*
—C. Joybell

I am blown away by the kindness, care and compassion we have received from so many people since Sharen suffered her stroke. When Sharen was in the hospital and subsequently the rehabilitation center, friends and family arranged meals for me over the course of numerous weeks. (These folks obviously recognized what a lost soul I was in the kitchen). Still today, when we visit the grocery store, church, restaurants and most other places, people are incredibly kind to Sharen and offer to help in a variety of ways. On more than one occasion, individuals have anonymously paid for our meals when Sharen and I were dining out. There truly is goodness in the world.

At the same time, there is a growing trend in our society in which some folks are increasingly intolerant of anyone who is different from them—whether it's in appearance, background, views and needs. We are losing the ability and the desire to see things from another person's viewpoint. This is causing a breakdown in communication, a surge in frustration and anger and the inability to work together for the good of everyone.

There is an erosion of empathy in the world. Empathy is the awareness of other people's feelings, how those feelings affect their needs and how they perceive a given set of circumstances. Empathy is not the same as sympathy. While sympathy is the feeling of pity for someone else's misfortune, empathy is more about your willingness to walk a mile in another person's shoes. It's about understanding what they are going through and sharing their feelings. It's about considering the prism through which someone views life when you decide how to relate to them or make a decision that affects them.

In Sharen's case, it seems the lack of empathy in the world affects her at some of the worst possible times. About two years after her stroke, Sharen, our daughter Nicole and I decided to take a winter break in Florida. Travelling can be a challenge for Sharen, and this trip got off to a rough start. We showed up at the airport on a brutally cold Saturday morning (hence the trip to a warmer climate). Unfortunately, the airline left us standing in a long line outside the terminal for more than an hour. Nicole and I moved Sharen indoors while we chilled (literally) with the rest of the passengers in the outside line.

That was bad enough, but the really tough part came as we went through security. Sharen was first in line and was quickly (and somewhat rudely) whisked off to the side by a TSA agent who was in quite a foul mood. Because we don't travel a lot, Sharen was confused by what was happening and quickly became emotional. Unfortunately, Nicole and I were stuck in line and couldn't rush over to comfort Sharen or lend her a hand. The TSA agent was not interested in our pleas to let us help. The situation deteriorated when the TSA agent could not understand why my wife was unable take off her shoes and refused to listen to Sharen's attempt at an explanation. (I've had a stroke—I need some help with this.) Then, the TSA agent started a not-so-gentle frisking of her body, which sent an emotionally-wracked Sharen over the edge. Finally, Nicole was freed from line and able to rush over to lend a hand, much to the dismay of the TSA agent who had no interest in trying to understand Sharen's challenges. A simple willingness to understand—which really should not have been that difficult—would have allowed us to avoid this unnecessarily unpleasant situation. If only the TSA agent had shown a little empathy.

Empathy always has been one of Sharen's finest character traits. She is very relatable, and people enjoy sharing their stories, concerns and challenges with Sharen. People are instinctively drawn to her, and they know that she genuinely cares about them. From Sharen's perspective, once a friend, always a friend.

In the same way, people will be drawn to you as a leader when you display genuine empathy. It is one of the most critically important leadership traits yet one that is often overlooked. Studies show having empathy in the workplace increases employee job satisfaction. However, more than half of employees feel there is a lack of empathy in their organization. In recent surveys of leading CEOs around the world, these executives say that empathy is one of the most important traits leaders will need in the coming years.

## WE'RE LOSING IT

Despite the empirical data that supports the importance of empathy, the trendline in society is moving in the wrong direction. Technology is not working in our favor. We are raising generations of people who are spending their lives with their faces buried in their phones. The thought of face-to-face conversations practically paralyzes many folks today. Even so, we need personal interaction to understand people's feelings. We have to see it in their faces, hear it in their voices, and detect it in their body language. You can't sense these feelings via text or e-mail. To make matters worse, social media makes it too easy for us to lash out at others, hiding behind our feeds—often in anonymity.

The decline in empathy goes much deeper than technology. There is an undercurrent of anger in our society that has been erupting like a volcano in recent years. This building anger has deepened rifts between us, increased polarization and caused a loss of civility. How many times have you read or heard stories where speakers at forums have been interrupted and shouted down by angry, disrespectful citizens who refuse to allow the speaker to finish? How many times have you seen news reports of public figures who are humiliated and forced to leave a restaurant rather than endure a vicious verbal assault from people who simply disagree with their beliefs? Unfortunately, it is happening all too often.

This brings to mind a situation involving TV talk show host Ellen DeGeneres. In 2019, DeGeneres (known for her more liberal viewpoints) was severely chastised on social media for sitting next to former President George W. Bush (who is notably more conservative) at a sporting event. DeGeneres went on her talk show the next day and explained that she and the former president are friends. Shouldn't that be enough? Why can't we be friends with people with whom we don't always agree? Why can't we enjoy a box of popcorn with someone who has different beliefs or perspectives? How will we ever solve complex problems if we can't even have a civil conversation with people who look and think differently than we do?

The loss of empathy in the world did not happen overnight. I first became aware of this disturbing trend during my years as a general manager of a local television station. It was not uncommon for people to call me when they were unhappy with one of the news stories we had aired. I also would receive frequent complaints about political advertising during election years. (I know, everybody hates those darn ads!) When digging down into the merits of the complaint, in almost 100 percent of the cases, the root cause of the viewer's unhappiness was the fact that they didn't want a public airing of positions with which they disagreed. Sure, we made our share of mistakes—but for the most part, people expected me to censure controversial speech simply because didn't like it. My answer to this complaint was simple: The way to address issues of speech is with more speech, not less. However, this response never satisfied a single caller.

We don't have to agree on everything. However, we have a responsibility to understand where another person is coming from. That is the only way we can reach some sort of common ground and move forward in a unified manner.

Many people have suggested to me that they cannot always empathize because they haven't had the same experiences and struggles as another person. Research professor and author Brené Brown offers a definition of empathy worth considering:

> *"Empathy is not connecting to an experience, it's connecting to the emotions that underpin an experience."*
> *(1)—Brené Brown*

In other words, you don't have to live through the same experiences as another person to empathize with them. For instance, while you may not have gone through a divorce, you have certainly experienced many of the emotions of those struggling with divorce—whether it is anger, bitterness, fear, anxiety, shame, etc. You can use that emotional connection to support your friends during these tough times.

When I served as a public relations consultant, one of my first clients was the United Way in my community. The organization had been victimized by a very large embezzlement scam that had occurred over a long period of time. News of the embezzlement rocked the community and eventually led to the resignation of the organization's CEO. The fallout from the scandal threatened the very existence of this great organization, which had done so much good for those in need for many decades. Would donors be willing to support an organization that had lost their trust?

The United Way hired my firm to help them through the crisis. The very first step we took was simple: We listened to all the various constituencies involved in the United Way network, including donors, agencies that depended on their financial support, volunteers, board members and the United Way staff, who were also victims of a very tragic set of circumstances. We held a number of sessions to listen to the voices of all those involved. We were able to hear the fears, frustrations, anger, disappointment and loss of trust that many people felt. We also heard voices say there was a path forward thanks to the many years of positive equity the United Way had established in the community. People also recognized the embezzlement was the work of one person and that the rest of the United Way team was filled with capable, competent, honest, hard-working staff who had a demonstrated a track record of seeking the best for those they served. Though there were hard feelings and concerns that were not easy to overcome, people were also willing to forgive as long as they saw a viable, transparent and sensible game plan going forward.

By connecting with the strong emotions of these people, we were able to develop a winning game plan to help the United Way rebuild trust before their next fundraising campaign. It was hard work for everyone involved. But not only did the United Way survive; the organization continues to thrive to this day. This local United Way continues to work tirelessly to make a major difference in the lives of thousands of people who are touched by their efforts.

## GET OUT OF YOUR BUBBLE

The deterioration of empathy in organizational culture is undermining the ability of companies to solve tough problems and stay ahead of the innovation curve. Leaders would be well-served if they sought first to understand others and then tapped into that understanding to reshape their approach to any given situation.

In the television newsroom, we faced a chronic challenge: ongoing conflicts between the news and engineering departments. Because news cameras and editing equipment were constantly in use, they frequently broke down—much to the chagrin of the news people who depended on the equipment to do their jobs and the engineers who were expected to repair it. It was a constant source of tension, and the interaction between the two departments was less than friendly. In fact, it often was downright hostile. News personnel felt the engineers did not provide customer friendly service and were slow to complete repairs. To make matters worse, the news folks were regularly frustrated when the same piece of equipment would break down again. Engineers felt the news personnel were overly demanding and abusive in their handling of the equipment. In fact, one chief engineer told me all videographers were goons.

In retrospect, both departments were made up of generally capable, competent professionals who wanted to do their best work. Everyone was equally frustrated. Also, there was a grain of truth in the viewpoints on both sides (excluding the part about goons, of course). We simply couldn't get these people to step out of their own bubble long enough to get inside anyone else's bubble.

At one of the newsrooms where I worked, we did achieve a bit of a breakthrough when the chief engineer left to work for another company. The assistant chief was promoted to the head position and immediately informed me that he was going to seek to improve relations between the two departments. We didn't exactly achieve world peace, but things improved markedly. In the process, I realized that despite working near this new chief engineer for a number of years, I didn't know him all that well. His willingness to try to work together and understand where other folks were coming from made a big difference in relations between the two departments.

Over time, I began to understand that one of the challenges between news people and engineers was the different make-up of the personalities involved. Engineers who I had always considered to be stand-offish were simply introverts. Once I reached that realization, I started to take the initiative to build better relations with them. Because they were introverts, I knew it had to be me to reach out and make that happen.

There was one engineer who was particularly grumpy. We'll say his name was Pete. One day, a member of the administrative staff was complaining that Pete never said hi to anyone. I asked her if she had ever said hi to him. Her response:

"Well, *no…*" (Insert a facial expression and tone of voice that communicated, "Why would I do that?")

Okay then.

From that point forward, every time I saw him, I made a point of always saying, "Hi, Pete." At first, he responded with a simple "Hi." After a few months, he started to say, "Hi, Ross." Every day as I was making my rounds, I also made a point to stop by engineering and talk with the team—no agenda involved, just conversation.

Years later, when I was leaving the station, a number of people had some very kind things to say to me. My favorite was from Pete, the grumpy engineer, who had worked at the station for more than three decades. He said:

"Of all the general managers who have ever walked the halls of this place, you were far and away the best."

All because I chose to say hi.

## A CULTURE OF EMPATHY BREEDS TRUST, COMMUNICATION, CREATIVE PROBLEM SOLVING & INNOVATION

Like all good leadership characteristics, empathy is contagious. Leaders who role model empathy will encourage other leaders and followers to embrace the same approach. Once empathy is hard-wired into your organizational culture, teams become closer, communication barriers break down and tough conversations become easier. This all leads to improved problem solving and an environment where innovation flourishes.

Here are a few of the great things an empathetic culture will do for your team:

### #1: Empathy bridges gaps between people.

Of course, we all have differences, whether it's gender, racial, ethnic, socio-economic, geographic or religious. All of these differences affect how we view the world. This diversity often divides us because when we interact with people who are different from us, we fail to see where they are coming from. This causes many to resist building more diverse organizations; people tend to hire people like themselves because they can relate to them. The better approach is to embrace differences in people and encourage those differences on our teams. If we are to develop the best solutions for our customers, we have to cultivate and celebrate a culture that reflects the rich diversity that exists in the world.

### #2: Empathy helps you understand the root cause of employee performance issues.

When it comes to evaluating employees, leaders are often wrong or simply unaware of what is going on. An employee on one of my teams was having difficulty arriving at work on time. This was affecting attitudes of others who felt she wasn't pulling her weight. When I had a sit down with her, I learned the root of the problem: The person who cared for her child could not arrive until later in the morning. We simply adjusted our team member's work schedule to give her a little later start time. Problem solved.

### #3: Empathy builds trust.

As you encourage people to share their feelings and viewpoints, you build a culture where all team members know they can safely share what's on their mind, even if it is a differing opinion. When people know it is okay to share openly and honestly with no judgment or recrimination, the bond of trust becomes stronger. Once you have reached this level of trust, *anything* is possible.

### #4: Empathy leads to better communication.

When trust exists, it's much easier to have tough conversations. In this climate, people are willing to disagree and hold each other accountable. They also are more open to constructive feedback because they understand it is not a personal attack, but rather coming from a place of what is best for the team. The best feedback occurs in a culture that has ongoing two-way communication.

### #5: Empathy leads to better solutions.

The more we encourage open dialogue and the expression of multiple viewpoints, the more good ideas will emerge. Even the best ideas are made better by healthy dialogue with multiple viewpoints. When teams have a genuine desire to consider other points of view, it helps to avoid groupthink and identify blind spots that often impede progress or cause initiatives to fail.

### #6: Empathy and innovation go hand-in-hand.

If you have trust, great communication and better solutions, innovation will flourish. Empathy allows you to better understand the needs of others, including your team members *and* your customers. In this rapidly changing world, the current needs of your customers will likely be very different six months from now. Your ability to step inside your customer's bubble will impact how effectively your team can design timely and innovative solutions to meet their needs.

So, what exactly does an organization with a culture of empathy look like? According to entrepreneur and author Michael Ventura, one of the first things you notice about these organizations is that their employees passionately engage in the company's overall mission and direction.

> *"People aren't simply coming to work to perform a specific function; they are showing up, in the broadest sense of the term, bringing their full self to the entirety of the business and its mission." (2)—Michael Ventura*

A culture of empathy leads to an alignment in vision throughout the organization. In 1961, President John F. Kennedy laid out an ambitious vision for the country when he pledged the U.S. would put a man on the moon by the end of the decade. A year later, President Kennedy was touring the NASA Launch Operations Center in Florida when, as the story goes, he encountered a janitor carrying a broom past the tour group. President Kennedy stopped the man and said, "Hi, I'm Jack Kennedy. What do you do here?" The man responded, "Well, I'm helping put a man on the moon." (3)

Now, that's alignment!

## BUILDING A CULTURE OF EMPATHY

Perhaps the most important trend in organizational culture in recent years has been a shift from the command and control style of management to a coaching culture. Instead of managers simply telling subordinates what to do, today's culture requires a team-based, collaborative approach in which managers coach their team members.

Throughout this book, I have written about the importance of listening. Good listeners share a common characteristic: they pick up on non-verbal cues. When you become an expert at recognizing the importance of what is *not* being said, this will allow you to connect with people on a deeper level. In my early days as a radio reporter, I covered the State Capitol on my daily beat. Our Capitol mailbox was flooded with news releases every day. The first thing I learned about news releases was that the people writing them only tell you what they want you know about a particular issue. Their hope is that the reporter will report the story exactly as it is written in the news release. My mentors taught me the importance of "reading between the lines" of these releases to get at the real story. Expert reporters learn to seek out the points of view not expressed in the news release, balance that with the viewpoint of the organization that issued the news release and report a balanced, complete news story.

As leaders, you are not always going to get the full story from your team. You have to be observant of body language that may indicate a particular employee is unhappy or disengaged. You may notice that someone's energy level is lower on a given day or their performance lags over a period of time. Being alert and probing these non-verbal cues will allow you to more rapidly identify problems at an early stage and connect with the emotions that lie beneath your team member's concerns or challenges.

If you want to encourage a culture where everyone is open, honest and vulnerable, you are going to have to go first. Be willing to share your feelings, interests and passions, even if doing so is against your nature. The only way you'll be able to connect emotionally within your team is by modeling the behavior you want to see in others.

This reminds me of the time I was brought in to coach a technology company executive who was struggling in her relationships with many of her peers. I conducted individual interviews with her supervisor, peer executives and direct reports. What I discovered was that her direct reports loved her while fellow executives felt she was defensive, self-serving and highly negative.

Upon probing deeper, I began to suspect this individual had a relatively low level of emotional intelligence. She was not aware of how the words and phrasing she chose were landing with other people. For example, she often started her questions with the word "why." During our coaching time, I explained that "why" makes people feel defensive and judged. A simple shift to starting questions with "what" or "how" would make a world of difference in the way she was perceived. Peers also felt she was self-serving and only cared about her own agenda, not theirs. Her direct reports had been exposed to the same behaviors, but over time came to understand that she was actually a very caring individual. This caused them to overlook some of her low EQ issues. Her peers weren't around her enough to make that same attitude shift.

I often encourage coaching clients to take an emotional intelligence assessment. One of my favorites can be found in the book *Emotional Intelligence 2.0* (TalentSmart 2009) by Travis Bradberry and Jean Greaves. The short online assessment will let you know where you stand in EQ compared to national averages in four areas: self-awareness, self-management, social awareness and relationship management. The book also offers 66 strategies to help boost your EQ scores. (4)

This particular client had fairly low social awareness and relationship management scores. She made a conscious effort to employ several strategies to help her improve in these areas, and I coached her regularly on them over a period of time. After six months, I interviewed her team members again and found their perception of her had improved dramatically—particularly among her peers and her supervisor. One significant shift was that her peers reported she was much better when it came to empathy—they felt she was taking more of a big picture approach and better understanding issues from their viewpoint. Her direct reports, who had always given her a good evaluation, also said they noticed a marked change in her leadership approach.

An empathic leadership style shows that you care. If you are willing to get inside the bubble of other people, especially those who are quite different from you, it can make everyone feel like a team and increase productivity, morale and loyalty. Empathy is a powerful tool that all great leaders must have in their leadership tool box.

## COACHING TIPS

**Coaching Tip #1:** Take an Emotional Intelligence assessment. Where are your best opportunities to increase your EQ?

**Coaching Tip #2:** Encourage the development of coaching skills on your team. Require team members to coach each other on a regular basis.

# LEADERSHIP INSIGHT #8:

# Encourage the Courage in Others

*"If you want to influence your peers, become their best cheerleader. Praise their strengths. Acknowledge their accomplishments. Say positive things about them to your boss and peers. Sincerely compliment them at every opportunity, and someday you may have the opportunity to influence them."—John C. Maxwell, The 360° Leader*

The first few weeks after Sharen returned home were arduous as she struggled to adjust her new reality. After she had been home for three weeks, we arranged for transportation so we could all attend church together on Christmas Eve. For our kids and me, it was a time for celebration, being able to have Christmas with Sharen at home. For Sharen, it was a melancholy experience. First of all, she felt uncomfortable at church. Then later, as the kids were playfully "fighting" in the kitchen, Sharen was resting in her hospital bed in her temporary bedroom. She lamented to me, "The kids are out there play-fighting, and I'm not in the center of it."

Heartbreaking.

Those first few weeks after Sharen returned home were also the most stressful for me as a caregiver. Suddenly, I had full-time responsibility for her care and well-being. No more health care professionals around 24 hours a day. I felt alone and afraid.

We were both in deep need of encouragement.

The first dose of encouragement came from Sharen's physical therapist. At the end of their first session, he made this matter-of-fact statement: "We'll get her up and walking."

Just the fact that he seemed to know this filled our hearts with hope. That was the positive boost we both needed. In the weeks ahead, Sharen did start walking, her speech began to return more fully and we were able to start taking trips to the store together. Life was looking up!

Over the next several months, I marveled at how all the professionals who worked with Sharen encouraged her progress, literally every step of the way. Though she wasn't able to regain all the activities she enjoyed before her stroke, like driving and negotiating steps, her quality of life improved immeasurably. I could visibly see how the daily doses of encouragement she received from her therapists, friends and family provided the positive boost she needed to keep working hard and making progress.

## ENCOURAGEMENT AND ITS PROFOUND
## IMPACT ON HISTORY

Other than Jesus, no individual has had a more profound impact on the history of Christianity than the Apostle Paul. Author of half of the New Testament, Paul's tenacity and leadership were instrumental in the growth of the Christian church in the 1st century and the spread of the gospel message over the past 2,000 years. The trials he endured during his ministry seem almost unimaginable:

"Five times I received from the Jews the forty lashes minus one. Three times I was beaten with rods, once I was stoned, three times I was shipwrecked, I spent a night and a day in the open sea, I have been constantly on the move. I have been in danger from rivers, in danger from bandits, in danger from my own countrymen, in danger from Gentiles, in danger in the city, in danger in the country, in danger at sea and in danger from false brothers. I have labored and toiled and often gone without sleep; I have known hunger and thirst and have often gone without food; I have been cold and naked." (1)—2 Corinthians 11:24-27

As strong, determined, disciplined and courageous as Paul was, he likely never would have been the leader he became had he not received encouragement in the very beginning of his journey from a man named Barnabas. When Paul began his ministry, many Christians distrusted him because of his background as a persecutor of those of the Christian faith. Barnabas was the only person willing to risk his own life to work with Paul and to convince others that Paul was the real deal. Barnabas, which stands for Son of Encouragement, stood by Paul as he developed his knowledge and honed his skills in preparation for the journey of a lifetime.

Who is your Barnabas? What role have they played in your success? For whom are *you* willing to play the role of Barnabas? You may not reshape history, but you could reshape a career if you are willing to encourage the courage in others during their journey.

## LEADERS MUST SHOW THE WAY

As a leader, it is important to model encouragement—not only to bring out the best in your team, but also to inspire peer-to-peer encouragement as a regular practice.

Steve Jobs is widely viewed as one of the greatest leaders of the technology generation. Yet many have forgotten that Jobs was once fired from Apple. He returned after the company experienced years of sluggish results. Upon his return, Jobs encouraged Apple team members to think of themselves as "creative innovators." The resulting turnaround is one of the legendary stories in contemporary business. Jobs' encouragement empowered the Apple team to innovate like never before in the company's history. The result was a series of revolutionary products: the iPod, iPad and iPhone, which literally changed the world and caused Apple's profits to soar.

Encouragement is a gift that leaders can offer. It doesn't cost you a dime, but the benefits can be enormous for each individual, the team as a whole and especially for you as a leader. There is no special talent required to provide encouragement. All it takes is the desire to bring out the best in others by encouraging positive behaviors, talents and attitudes you see in them.

During my years in the television news business, it was common practice for us to hire several college interns each semester. Our station was located near a major university with a robust communications college, so the supply of talented interns was plentiful. We used the internships to develop reporters who in many cases ended up joining our team as paid reporters.

Our team was particularly impressed with one intern who displayed all of the attributes necessary for success: good work ethic, positive attitude, energy, enthusiasm and a desire to improve. Though we wanted to add this particular intern to our team, we had no openings on our staff when she graduated. She moved back home, about an hour from our station, and was hired for a part-time job at a local radio station.

Several months passed and we finally had a part-time opening for a reporter working the evening shift. The job paid a minimal wage.

Financially, it was not a good move for her, as she would have to drive an hour each way and keep her morning job in radio to make ends meet. Most young people would have declined the opportunity in favor of more sleep. But this young woman's desire to break into television was so strong that she took the job, kept her radio gig and drove two hours every day for several months.

Eventually, a full-time position opened up on our team and she was promoted into that role. Through the years, she continued to work as hard or harder than anyone on our team, grew her skills and eventually moved on to the anchor desk. Thirty years later, Sheri Jones remains one of the premier news anchors in the region and one of the most recognized and beloved personalities in the community.

Quite frankly, Sheri has earned everything her career has brought her. I had practically nothing to do with her growth, other than recognizing her talent and encouraging her development and growth through the years. Most interesting is how much encouragement she has given back to me by continually thanking me and crediting me (more than I deserve) for her success. Encouragement definitely cuts both ways!

## ENCOURAGE THROUGH AFFIRMATION

One of the best ways leaders can encourage team members is through simple words of affirmation. Loads of research shows that employees who feel affirmed work harder, are more productive and are more likely to remain with the organization. On the flip side, more than half workers who quit their job say they left in large part because they felt unappreciated. The bottom line is that employees need to be appreciated for what they do, according to Gary Chapman and Paul

White, authors of *The 5 Languages of Appreciation in the Workplace: Empowering Organizations by Encouraging People* (Northfield Publishing 2019).

> *"We believe people in the workplace need to feel*
> *appreciated in order for them to enjoy their job, do their*
> *best work, and continue working over the long haul." (2)*
> —*Gary Chapman & Paul White*

"Employees overwhelmingly choose receiving Words of Affirmation as the primary way they like to be shown appreciation in the workplace," write Chapman and Paul. "Almost half of all employees (over 45%) prefer receiving verbal praise as their primary language of appreciation." (3)

It is simple and it works. No fancy plaques or dinners required (although those are nice, too). Just genuine, heartfelt words of affirmation. That's all it takes. Here are a few examples:

"Thank you for your work on that presentation. It made the difference in completing the sale."

"Thanks to your extra effort in completing the project, we made our deadline and the final result was noticeably better than our competition."

"You have faced a lot of challenges and overcome many obstacles to complete this task. Congratulations on a job very well done."

"You are the consummate team player. I appreciate your willingness to listen to others and the encouragement you give to those around you."

"Thanks for bringing your best to work every day."

If you are not in the practice of delivering affirmation, I'll admit, it will feel awkward at first. But here's a helpful tip: keep it real. If your words are not authentic, your team will know. A simple "thank you for a job well done" is a great starting point. Much like exercising a muscle, you will get stronger as you work at it.

## ENCOURAGE THEIR CONFIDENCE

There is a fine line between confidence and a lack of confidence. I am always amazed at the number of supremely successful people in all walks of life who from time-to-time express a lack of confidence. In the sports world, I've noticed a common pattern: when a team is on a losing streak, inevitably a news story comes out quoting a player saying, "We're not playing with a lot of confidence right now." I always wonder how some of the most exceptionally conditioned and talented athletes could ever lack confidence in their ability, but they often do.

In the business world, there is a well-documented characteristic known as the Imposter Syndrome. This is when highly successful people who have been promoted many times in their career worry that people will begin to recognize they are not really as good as their reputation suggests. The Imposter Syndrome has derailed a number of successful careers.

As a leader, you are surrounded by people with varying levels of confidence. You can help boost their confidence by empowering them with challenging assignments, which shows you trust them. Celebrate and affirm their success. Reinforce their positive behaviors by acknowledging how those behaviors are allowing the team to be more successful. In many cases, building awareness of their many positive accomplishments, both personally and professionally, can be the best confidence boost of all.

I recently coached an IT executive who was struggling with internal relationships at work. My heart goes out to IT people who are overloaded with endless technology problems across the organization and have numerous customers who all feel their IT issue should be top priority. This poor soul was experiencing that predicament. He was getting negative reviews from people who felt he was too slow to respond and fix things, and he was receiving negative evaluations from his supervisors who were hearing the complaints. He was naturally introverted, which made him seem distant and uncaring to some. Understandably, these circumstances caused a serious erosion in his confidence.

During coaching, we focused on a couple of key issues, including how he was communicating with others and his self-image—how he was presenting himself in individual conversations and meetings. Those were pretty easy fixes, and in a couple of weeks people began commenting to him on the positive changes they were noticing. A longer-term tactic we employed was getting him to establish and write down goals. Achieving goals and celebrating those victories go a long way in building confidence.

When coaching around confidence, I often ask clients to complete what I call an achievement log. This is exactly what it sounds like: a list of everything you have achieved in your life, both professional and personal. I ask my clients to take an hour to reflect on and write down all of their accomplishments, including education, family, career advancements, certifications and personal highlights. I have done this myself and encourage you to do the same. We have all accomplished a lot more in our lives than we usually give ourselves credit for.

After this IT executive completed his achievement log, we spent the next coaching session reviewing everything on his list. It was quite impressive. As we neared the end of the coaching session, I asked for permission to make an observation, which I posed in the form of a question: "How could anyone who has achieved all of this ever have a problem with confidence?" He smiled with eyes open wide and nodded quietly in agreement. I encouraged him to keep his list, regularly review it and update it. I do this myself when I feel my confidence waning, and it never fails to lift me up.

## ENCOURAGE THROUGH FAILURE

How you treat failure speaks volumes about you as a leader. Failure is the doorway through which we all have to walk if we want to achieve success. As a leader, if you reprimand team members and take away opportunities as a result of failure, you will demotivate them, squash innovation and lose great talent. People will only realize their full potential if they have the freedom to fail and are encouraged to learn from their mistakes and get better as a result.

One of the most highly regarded presidents in American history, Abraham Lincoln, had a long list of failures in his lifetime that would have squashed the advancement of most ambitious people.

| | |
|---|---|
| Lost job/Defeated for State Legislature | 1832 |
| Failed in business | 1833 |
| Nervous breakdown | 1836 |
| Defeated for Speaker | 1838 |
| Defeated for nomination for Congress | 1843 |
| Lost re-nomination | 1848 |
| Rejected for land officer | 1849 |
| Defeated for nomination for Vice President | 1856 |
| Again defeated for U.S. Senate | 1858 |
| Elected President | 1860 |

Most of us would not be able to push forward as Lincoln did in the face of that many failures. However, we are more likely to move forward if those around us, especially our leaders, recognize and encourage us to continue to develop our abilities, using failure to grow and not withdraw. (4)

## EMPOWER AND TRUST

Team members will feel encouraged when you empower them to do their jobs and when they know you truly trust them to manage the work. All too often, leaders pay lip service to empowerment and then proceed to micromanage the details of a project. That is the opposite of empowerment!

When a vice president for a large commercial construction company was struggling to adjust to his new role in management, his supervisor sent him to me for coaching. The executive had spent much of his career as a project director, a role in which he excelled. In his new position of vice president, he was overseeing the work of all the other project directors in the company.

As often is the case in these types of situations, instead of empowering his project directors to manage each individual project, the newly promoted executive wanted to engage himself in many of the day-to-day details of each project. This happens quite often in organizational culture. People get promoted because of the good work they have done, and they don't want to relinquish the tasks they have been successful at and enjoy. However, this vice president's micro-management was causing morale among the highly talented team of project directors to plummet.

Through our coaching engagement, the vice president came to understand that in his new role, he should be more of an oversight person and a resource for the project directors when they needed help. He soon began to shift from behaviors that discouraged his team to a role that was more supportive and encouraging.

## ENCOURAGE THE COURAGE ACROSS THE FINISH LINE

Sian Welch was nearing the finish line in the 1997 Ironman Triathlon in Hawaii. Her body had run out of fuel, and her systems were shutting down. Less than 100 feet from the finish line of the grueling event, she collapsed. Struggling to get to her feet, she collapsed several more times. Coming right behind her was Wendy Ingraham who collided with Sian and also fell down near the finish line. The two literally crawled across the finish line, Wendy finishing just ahead of Sian.

In the ultimate act of sportsmanship, Wendy reached her hand out to a desperately struggling Sian and pulled her across the finish line.

There will be many moments in your leadership career when people around you are desperately in need of courage to move forward. They may lack confidence or be deeply fearful of failure. They may lack the vision they need to see the finish line. Or they may need a small affirmation to brighten their day or their outlook. In these situations, every one of us needs leaders who encourage the courage that exists inside us.

You may never know how simple, daily doses of encouragement could make a difference in someone's life. Rest assured, someday someone will reach out to you, maybe years later, and say, "Thank you for the encouragement."

## COACHING TIPS

**Coaching Tip #1:** Make a list of all the things you appreciate about each of your team members. Share it with them.

**Coaching Tip #2:** Ask each of your team members to complete an achievement log. Review it together.

# LEADERSHIP INSIGHT # 9:

# Overcome Life's Challenges with Resilience

*"The ultimate measure of a man is not where he stands
in moments of comfort and convenience, but where he
stands at times of challenge and controversy."*
—*Dr. Martin Luther King*

Sometimes life throws us a detour. It would be helpful if we could see a sign that says "Detour Ahead" so we would have time to prepare. Unfortunately, it doesn't work that way. Detours are thrust upon us, usually with no advance knowledge and we are forced to take an alternative route.

Since her stroke, it seems as if Sharen has encountered one detour after another. In the years following the stroke, she had to fight through the challenges of therapy until she eventually reached her "new normal" in terms of her mobility and lifestyle. She had to adjust to a loss of independence, the inability to drive and having to depend on me for things that she had done all her life, such as opening containers and packages when cooking meals. She fought through the pain of losing precious relationships because she was limited in where she could go. Through it all she persevered. She adjusted and adapted. She always maintained her positive spirit. She fought and battled because she loves life and loves her family.

Just about the time we started to feel a sense of smooth sailing in our lives, another detour popped up. Cancer. Sharen was diagnosed with endometrial cancer, which required ten months of therapy: first chemotherapy followed by radiation treatments. She endured more battles, suffered the loss of her hair, had to deal with more fear and uncertainty and face endless trips to the hospital. Thankfully, she emerged cancer free!

Shortly after the cancer, her ailing left shoulder deteriorated to the point that she was in constant pain. She could not even lift her arm to place a coffee cup in the cupboard or reach the microwave. She needed a new shoulder. The recovery from shoulder replacement surgery was more challenging for Sharen than it is for most patients because she could not endure any weight bearing on her left arm for six weeks. That was her good arm, which meant no walking for a month and a half since she could not lean on her walker. Once again, she battled through the obstacles and now enjoys almost full range of motion in her shoulder—and she's pain-free.

Sharen has endured plenty of other challenges, including diabetes, osteoporosis and high blood pressure. If there is one characteristic that has enabled her to pull through all of life's hurdles, it is her resilience. She responds to adversity with a determined will to overcome and emerge strong. Life may not be what it used to be for Sharen. However, in some respects, the challenges she has endured has given her and all of us around her a new perspective and drawn us closer together. This has helped Sharen and our family develop a much deeper appreciation for what really matters in life.

Resilience is the ability to adapt to life's misfortunes and setbacks. It is the ability to roll with the punches. Resilient leaders are able to harness their inner strength, allowing themselves and their teams to rebound from setbacks and deal with challenges.

## TOUGH TIMES ARE AN OPPORTUNITY FOR GROWTH

Your growth as a leader will never be a straight-line upward trajectory. You will face numerous setbacks, difficult challenges and seemingly insurmountable odds that cause your growth curve to flatten. This is where resilience comes into play. When others are collapsing under the burdens of frustrations and disappointment, resilience will give you the vision to see a path forward. With resilience, you'll know the change brought about by tough times will make you and the team stronger and put you in a better position to compete as you emerge from short-term challenges. Often, leaders are defined by how they handle the crises in life. Your team looks to you for your guidance, and they will model your behavior based on how you deal with difficult times.

Tough times also present leaders with an opportunity for self-reflection. This could potentially lead to positive changes in who you are, how you lead and what direction you will head next in life. There have been three defining events in the 21st century that have impacted every person in the world in some fashion. The terrorist attacks of September 11, 2001 changed life forever. The devastating images of the collapse of the World Trade Center and the horrific loss of lives stunned our nation and the world. In many ways, we will never recover from this tragedy.

In the aftermath of 9/11, our nation had to face the reality that we would never be the same. We had to embrace a new way of living in a world that was less safe and secure. Leaders worked together to implement necessary changes, and for a period of time, we set aside political barriers and viewed life as Americans.

Most of us who lived through this time also did our own individual soul-searching. In 2001, my colleague and friend Dr. David Chinsky was in the midst of a highly successful 20-year career in corporate America. After serious reflection following 9/11, David decided the best contribution he could make to the world was to leave the safety of his lucrative corporate job and set up his own consulting firm dedicated to building great leaders. David established the Institute for Leadership Fitness and developed the Fit Leader's Program™. Thousands of people have completed his program and sing the praises of how it has positively impacted their careers. It has been my privilege to not only know David, but to work with him and become a certified life fitness instructor and facilitator of the program.

The second defining event of this century was the great recession that lasted from 2007 to 2011. I had lived through three previous recessions, and this was by far the worst. Many said it was the most devastating recession since the Great Depression of the 1930s. During this recession, the domestic automotive and housing industries collapsed. In Michigan, where I live, there was a loss of one million manufacturing jobs over the first decade of this century.

During this time, I was struggling to make ends meet in the public relations field. In the midst of the economic downturn, businesses were closing, merging or implementing deep cuts just to survive. It was not the best time to land the new clients I needed to pay my bills. To make ends meet, I decided I would have to provide an additional service. I didn't know what that service would be, but I knew it should be something I was good at and passionate about— and something that would make a difference in other people's lives. One day, I was discussing this with a colleague. In an effort to help me sort things out, she asked me what I had done that I really enjoyed and excelled at in my career. I mentioned how much I enjoyed mentoring young reporters during my time in television. She suggested that I look into coaching.

I had no real knowledge of what coaching entailed, but I decided to do my due diligence. I hired a coach for myself, enrolled in a coaching school and eventually became a credentialed coach. Soon after, I began one-on-one coaching, which eventually led me to leadership development and training programs, which I have enjoyed immensely. This is the path that led me to where I am today. This work is by far the most rewarding of anything I have ever done in the professional field. I often tell people it is like getting paid to do my hobby. And it all started with my determination to fight through tough times. It took resilience for me to stick with the training, the financial expense and the ramp-up time it took to make that portion of my business profitable.

As I write this chapter on resilience, the world is going through the third defining event of this young century: the COVID-19 pandemic. This unprecedented crisis swept through our nation and world in a shockingly vicious manner, leaving a horrifying mark of destruction. Families were devasted by sudden deaths of loved ones, the healthcare system was burdened to near collapse and businesses were shuttered (in some cases never to open again) as we sheltered-in-place as a society.

The concern over the health and safety of our loved ones and our communities was the highest priority during the COVID-19 crisis. The other significant fallout was the number of people who were furloughed from their jobs as organizations' operations were curtailed or shut down completely. I had family members who were laid off and struggled to pay their bills. My own business in leadership training took a significant short-term setback as organizations postponed or cancelled trainings. Though I felt fortunate to have a job, my monthly income dropped by more than a third during this time and took quite a while to recover.

I have seen numerous periods in my life when things were turned upside down. As I have grown older, I find that I am much calmer in the face of disaster. As we progressed through the COVID-19 pandemic, I found comfort knowing that the tough times would end someday—and the best way to deal with the crisis was to use the downtime to prepare for tomorrow.

Like most Americans, I worked remotely for several weeks during COVID-19. Fortunately, I actually had work to do, for which I felt grateful. I also had quite a bit of downtime. So, I intentionally developed a strategy to use that downtime for personal development. My biggest project was working on this book, which I aggressively advanced during this time. Before the pandemic, I also had been interested in breaking into the speaking business. I had a presentation that needed to be upgraded, a project that had been on the backburner because of my work on this book. I refined my presentation and developed some slides to go with it. Finally, as a credentialed coach I am required to have a certain number of continuing education credits. I used my time working remotely to secure several credits so I wouldn't have to worry about that when business started to pick up again.

Resilient leaders have the ability to rally their teams during a crisis. They can communicate a clear vision for not only how they will survive the tough times, but also for how they will thrive in the future. If you are that leader, your team will embrace your vision and rally behind you to make it happen.

## DON'T BOUNCE BACK. BOUNCE FORWARD.

If you hope to lead others through adversity, you must be resilient yourself. That begins with changing the way you think about adversity. Resilient leaders spend very little time looking backwards to pinpoint the cause of an event and quickly shift into forward-thinking response strategies. Resilient leaders don't waste time complaining about what they cannot control. They instead focus on what they can control and adjust accordingly.

Eric Greitens is a former Navy Seal and author of the book *Resilience: Hard-Won Wisdom for Living a Better Life* (Mariner Books 2015). He tells the story of a former Seal colleague who was diagnosed with Post Traumatic Stress Syndrome (PTSD) and battling alcoholism. The book features a series of letters that Greitens and his former colleague write to each other. According to Greitens, people often think resilience is about recovery or bouncing back. He says this mindset will cause us to miss out on what pain and suffering have to teach us. We can't undo the mistakes of the past because they have become part of who we are. Instead, Greitens encouraged his former colleague to accept who he was and not go back in time. (1)

> *"What happens to us becomes part of us. Resilient people do not bounce back from hard experiences; they find heathy ways to integrate them into their lives. In time, people find that great calamity met with great spirit can create great strength."—Eric Greitens*

In her book, *Option B: Facing Adversity, Building Resilience, and Finding Joy* (Knopf 2017), Sheryl Sandberg writes about dealing with the tragic loss of her husband. She says psychologists traditionally believed that people faced two possible outcomes of trauma: they either fell into depression, anxiety or PTSD, or they were resilient and bounced back to the state they were before their trauma. Sandberg's friend and co-author Adam Grant told her about post-traumatic growth and shared some research that showed half the people who experience a traumatic event report at least one positive change. Initially, Sandberg dismissed the idea as she struggled to live day-to-day in the months after her husband's death. But over time, she started to develop a new perspective. She found herself gaining appreciation and feeling grateful for what she had in life. She found greater meaning in life, especially in her work as COO of Facebook. She became open to new possibilities. She was bouncing forward. (2)

Recovering from tragic circumstances in not an overnight shift. It's a slow, difficult process. As a leader, you need to integrate the tough times into the DNA of your team, learn from it and bounce forward to a new, better reality.

## TOUGH TIMES ARE AN OPPORTUNITY TO PULL PEOPLE TOGETHER

When Winston Churchill delivered his famous "Never Give Up" speech to Harrow School students on October 29, 1941, Great Britain was experiencing its darkest days. In the midst of World War II, Germany had unleashed a series of vicious bombing attacks that destroyed much of Great Britain and left the nation feeling defeated. Was it over? Was there any chance for a recovery? Should Britain surrender to the Germans? A cause that appeared hopeless to much of the world was seen by Churchill as an opportunity to pull his nation together. He said:

"But for everyone, surely, what we have gone through in this period - I am addressing myself to the School - surely from this period of ten months this is the lesson: *never give in, never give in, never, never, never, never - in nothing, great or small, large or petty - never give in except to convictions of honour and good sense. Never yield to force; never yield to the apparently overwhelming might of the enemy.* We stood all alone a year ago, and to many countries it seemed that our account was closed, we were finished." (3)

Churchill did not follow conventional thinking or cave in to the intense political and military pressure he was feeling from all sides. He stood strong in his convictions. He stuck to his values. He inspired a nation and a world to persevere against all odds. As he ended his historic speech that day, he urged his nation to reframe how they viewed their crisis:

"Do not let us speak of darker days: let us speak rather of sterner days. These are not dark days; these are great days - the greatest days our country has ever lived; and we must all thank God that we have been allowed, each of us according to our stations, to play a part in making these days memorable in the history of our race." (4)

When times get tough, it is human nature to wallow in defeatism. That is why leaders are needed to rise above the negativism and the "woe is me" attitude that often prevails. As a leader, you need to stand firm in your conviction, adjust and adapt, and communicate a vision for the future that gets your team excited about new possibilities and a better tomorrow.

## TAKE CARE OF YOURSELF

Navigating a crisis is an extremely taxing ordeal. It takes a toll emotionally and physically. During these times, you may lose sleep, slip out of your regular exercise routine and turn to unhealthy snacks and fast food. That's okay in the short term, but after a while you will lose your ability to sustain your best self.

Headquartered in Lansing, Michigan, The Neogen Corporation is a world-leader in food and animal safety products. They have been recognized several times as one of Forbes 200 Best Small Companies in America and by Fortune Magazine as one the country's fastest growing small businesses. Like most successful companies, life in the early days wasn't always so glamorous for Neogen.

Neogen's retired COO Lon Bohannon once shared a story with me from the early days when the company was struggling to make payroll. Lon and CEO Jim Herbert were working 16-hour days, crisscrossing the country looking for additional financial backing. The president of a venture capital company that had invested in Neogen came to town one day and took Lon and Jim out to dinner. The investor could tell the pair of Neogen executives were exhausted and offered this insight:

"The companies we see that don't make it don't fail because they lack expertise, drive or even financial backing. They fail because their leaders burn out."

The risk of burnout is greater today than at any time in our lifetime. Everyone is doing more with less. The pace is faster, the pressure of change is constant, and with today's technology we are plugged in 24/7. We are bombarded with messages by text, phone and e-mail. The list of commitments we make to our bosses, colleagues, family and friends seems never-ending. Before long, a sense of overwhelming overload begins to take over our lives. If you do not take steps to mitigate these realities, you won't be the leader your team needs when times get really tough. You eventually will burn out.

When I ask leaders to inventory how they are doing when it comes to nutrition, exercise and rest, every single person can identify at least one thing they could start doing better today. That is my challenge to you: Take a hard look at how you are eating. What commitment could you make today that would improve your eating habits? For me, I should give up that extra cup of coffee that I don't really need. Put one new good habit into effect today and work on it for the next 21 days. Then, build in another new good habit.

As far as exercise, the most important thing is to find something you enjoy. Walk. Ride a bike. Swim. Add more movement in your life. You don't have to a gym membership to make a difference when it comes to exercise. For some, it helps to have an exercise partner. This also brings accountability into the picture because your exercise buddy will keep you on track. I always encourage people to first commit to a small, manageable step and then build on it. If you can commit to walking 20 minutes at lunch three times a week, do that and stick to it. You can add more later, after you have developed your new, healthy habit.

You also must take care of yourself by making sure you get plenty of rest and rejuvenation. First, schedule periods of time each week when you unplug from technology. This is a hard one for a lot of folks, however it is essential. Every time you look at an e-mail, voice mail or text on your day off, you are taking yourself right back to the stress of work, thereby negating the benefits of having a relaxing day off. There is a principle known as oscillation, which is the variation between two or more states. Your body requires that you balance those periods of energy expenditure with periods of rest. I compare it to recharging a battery. Get away from the technology. If you can't do it for an entire day, make a commitment to unplug for a half a day. Again, start with something manageable, commit and add to it later.

It also is essential to take regular days off. This can be hard, particularly during a crisis, but the payoffs are enormous. Set boundaries around your free time. Let people know you are going to be off and assign other people to cover your responsibilities. Develop a culture where everyone respects each other's free days. Your team will have greater, more consistent energy as a result.

Finally, you need to get 7 to 8 hours of sleep per night. I regularly ask people in my leadership trainings to raise their hands if they are getting 7 to 8 hours of sleep. I would estimate only about 25 percent of every class raises their hands. There are several cycles of sleep, the last of which is the most beneficial, REM or rapid eye movement. We hit the REM cycle about every 90 minutes. If you are not getting 7 to 8 hours of sleep per night, you are missing one REM cycle every night. That may not seem like a big deal—and it really isn't in the short-term. However, it will catch up to you later in life if you don't get enough sleep over the long-term.

If you take care of yourself through proper rest, exercise and nutrition, you will have the strength and energy to perform at a high level throughout your career. You will be a better you for everyone in your life, at work and at home. And you will have the full measure of resilience you need to lead your team through tough times.

## KEEP THINGS IN PERSPECTIVE

As I have helped Sharen deal with her challenges over the years, I've become more sensitized to the many people in this world who face every day obstacles. Perhaps I had been so selfishly living in my own world for much of my life, I had been unaware of how many people deal with various disabilities. I've also been struck by the realization that no matter what challenge we are facing on a given day, someone else has it worse than we do. This really hit home when Sharen was going through radiation treatments for cancer.

Because radiation must be given at the same time every day, we found ourselves sitting with the same people every day for several weeks. We all became like an extended family and learned each other's stories. While Sharen was going through radiation, there were some who were going through radiation and chemotherapy at the same time. Several people were dealing with a reoccurrence of cancer. There were a couple of self-employed individuals who were unable to work because the chemo was incapacitating them. One of them was a farmer who had a crop in the field he was unable to harvest because he was too sick. Fortunately, a neighbor helped him and his family out.

Resilient leaders need to put things in perspective when dealing with tough times. Some of your team members will use challenges as an excuse to fail. Don't accept these excuses. Instead, explain that the current challenges are short-term and how together your team will find innovative ways to pull through.

When you maintain an optimistic perspective, it doesn't mean you have to be Pollyannaish. Ignoring challenges or pretending they don't exist can be just as harmful as allowing those challenges to defeat you. During my years in television, economic downturns made it difficult to reach our sales goals. After a time, it was easy for sales people to blame the economy for everything. My approach wasn't to ignore the fact the economy was bad, but rather to encourage the team to look for potential new clients who were doing well in the downturn: attorneys, doctors, dentists, insurance professionals and others. Resilient leaders know that behind every dark cloud is a silver lining. Those new clients you develop today will still be with you long after the crisis is over.

Towards the tail end of the 2007-2011 recession, I ran into a friend who also happens to be one of the most successful residential real estate professionals in our area. Real estate had taken a huge beating in the recession, and a number of sales people had left the business. My friend's business was flourishing, but she acknowledged that it hadn't been easy. I asked what the key to her success had been during those tough times. Of course, she said hard work had been essential—but she also said she had to go back to the basics. This was something a lot of veteran real estate professionals who had enjoyed success for a number of years did not want to do. Going back to the basics meant selling lower-priced homes, which often came with more problems and buyers who had a harder time qualifying for a mortgage. Back to the basics meant more of what I call the "dirt under the nails" work that many people would rather not handle. My friend demonstrated great resilience during the economic downturn, and as a result, she continues to be successful at a very high level today. I am willing to bet that many of the people she helped buy or sell a home during that difficult time have been return customers and continue to be a source of more business for her today.

## DEVELOP A RESILIENT CRISIS PLAN

The best way to manage tough times is to be prepared for them before they occur. The worst time to develop a crisis plan is the moment the crisis occurs. When my firm started working with the local United Way following an embezzlement controversy, the non-profit made a few missteps that set them back even farther in the community. They did not have a crisis plan to guide them. After we successfully guided them through a tough year, I helped them write a crisis plan. Since that time, I have written a few crisis plans, always for organizations that did not have one when the turbulence started. I always cite Warren Buffet's quote to CEOs: "It can take 20 years to build a reputation and only five minutes to ruin it."

The reason most organizations don't have a crisis plan is because it doesn't seem urgent enough to demand attention—until a crisis strikes. This is a good strategic planning exercise for your team. If you don't have a crisis plan, make it a priority to develop one. If you do have a plan, make sure you regularly review and update it. Important contact information should be updated frequently. Changes in technology will impact how you execute various components of your plan.

If you have a good crisis plan in place, your team will be able to respond quickly, communicate clear, consistent messages and maintain trust with all your key stakeholders.

Resiliency won't make your problems go away. However, it does give you the ability to see beyond the immediate challenges, identify new directions and successfully convince your team to embrace each battle with passion and conviction—and ultimately come out on top.

**COACHING TIPS**

**Coaching Tip #1:** Make a list of things that add to or subtract from your resilience. Think about the difference between the two categories. What steps can you take to increase your resilience?

**Coaching Tip #2:** Imagine a time in the near future when everything is going well. Then identify what you need to do to make that happen.

# LEADERSHIP INSIGHT #10:

# Develop Everyone to Their Fullest Potential

*"What lies behind us and what lies before us are tiny matters compared with what lies within us."—Ralph Waldo Emerson*

After the first few life-threatening days following Sharen's stroke, my thoughts predominantly revolved around what quality of life she would enjoy in the long-term. What was her full potential for recovery? Would she speak? Would she walk? Would she even smile? Would she enjoy the things that have always been important in her life: family, friends, serving others and, most important to her, laughing?

Developing her potential was definitely a team effort. First, there was a tremendous team of therapists who worked with her at the hospital, in the nursing home, at our home and on an outpatient basis. I was so impressed with the skill this team of professionals demonstrated throughout the process. Not only were they experts in their field as far as their knowledge and execution of physical, occupational and speech therapy; but they also helped Sharen develop her potential through constant encouragement, patience and, when necessary, challenging her to do more than she thought she was capable of.

The support of family and friends was also instrumental in Sharen's recovery. The encouragement people offered through phone calls, prayers, cards, visits, e-mails and meals filled our hearts with joy and strengthened Sharen as she fought her battle.

Finally, Sharen's strong will and belief in herself played a major role in her recovery. She set lofty goals and maintained a positive attitude in the face of seemingly endless hours of therapy and individual workouts at home. She never would have developed her potential as much as she did without a personality that causes her to wake up every day with a smile and a willingness to push forward—even when she was sometimes tempted to take a day off.

Potential means that you have the ability to reach heights far greater than where you stand today. If you want to develop your potential, you may have to disregard popular opinion and push boundaries you've never broken through.

In the 1950s, several premier track athletes around the world made it their primary goal to break the four-minute mile. Many tried. None succeeded. Some became convinced it was impossible for a human to break the 4-minute barrier. It turned out that the barrier was more psychological than physical.

On May 6, 1954, Roger Bannister, a 25-year-old medical student from Oxford, England, crossed the one-mile finish line in 3:59.4. Once Bannister beat the 4-minute mile, several others followed suit over the next few years. Bannister refused to believe the "impossible boundary" of the 4-minute mile could not be crossed. His dogged determination, relentless training and pursuit of excellence encouraged others to do the same.

# RECOGNIZING POTENTIAL IN OTHERS

As a young adult, I had a burning desire for a career in radio. I charted my course in a bit of an unconventional manner. I first obtained a license from the Federal Communications Commission, something that was required in those days. Then, I was determined to land my first job. I faced a few challenges. I did not yet have a college degree. I had no experience, and unlike most people entering the field, I did not have a resume tape to showcase my talents. On top of all that, my image needed quite a bit of work. My hair was too long, and being poor, I didn't have the best clothes. I cleaned myself up pretty good, but I have to say all things considered I doubt that I would have hired me!

Given all of my shortcomings, I determined my only chance to land a radio job was with the small-town radio stations in the region where I lived. I identified five of those stations and set out to meet the owners of each. The results were, to put it mildly, deflating. One station owner was gracious enough to spend a half hour with me offering advice. The rest basically told me to forget about it. I saw no possibility of employment at any of the stations. Except one.

The last station I visited was WRBJ in St. Johns, Michigan. I happened to walk in the door just as the owner, Bob Ditmer, was coming off-the-air. We chatted for a few moments, and then he surprised me by saying he MIGHT have something part-time opening up in a few weeks. I was flying high with excitement after I left that day!

Over the next few months, I periodically dropped by the station, always when I knew Bob was getting off-the-air. Finally, he offered me a position—it was 10 hours a week, basically running the control board for other people. I thought I had gone to heaven. After a couple of months, Bob let me take over part of his morning shift. Of course, I realized I was only getting the position because Bob didn't like getting up at 5 am, not because of my talent, but it didn't matter to me. It was my opportunity to launch my career in broadcasting, one that lasted 27 years.

Bob Ditmer saw something in me that no one else recognized. I am not sure exactly what he saw, but his willingness to take a chance on an unimpressive rookie with no experience made all the difference in whether I even had a shot at a career in broadcasting. I had potential. It needed to be developed. I owe a strong debt of gratitude to Bob for the opportunity of a lifetime.

If you are willing to look beyond what others see and dig a little deeper to recognize true potential in others, you are taking the first step in helping them unleash their talent. This will allow them to break through barriers that that have been blocking them from realizing all they are capable of achieving.

## DEVELOPING OTHERS IS GOOD BUSINESS

When leaders are committed to helping others develop their potential, it's good for business. If those around us develop their full potential, they produce more for our organization and our teams become more productive. Consequently, our teams operate more cohesively, and our bottom line reflects those results. Even better? Research shows us leadership focused on developing talent increases employee engagement.

Oftentimes when I speak to business owners and C-Suite executives about development-related issues, I am asked about return on investment. Smart business people want to measure the results, as they should. The bottom line is this: developing talent is good for your bottom line. Frankly, I believe it is the best investment you can make for many reasons. Statistic after statistic confirms that developing employees leads to a dramatic net positive when it comes to engagement, productivity, talent acquisition and retention, sales, income and profits.

Employees with higher levels of engagement are 78 percent more productive and 40 percent more profitable for companies. Multiple surveys also show a correlation between engagement and higher sales and profit margins. For instance, a Dale Carnegie study showed that companies with engaged workers say their employees are 62 percent more productive and strongly agree that 61 percent of their customers are more satisfied. (1) In multiple surveys, when employees are asked what is most important to them about where they choose to work, development is at or near the top of the list and always ahead of financial considerations.

The longer you can keep good talent, the less you will have to invest in turnover. Employee turnover is incredibly costly—not only in terms of the hiring and training new employees, but also because it decreases productivity and employee engagement, which leads to lower profits.

## WHY DEVELOPMENT DOES NOT HAPPEN

Though most leaders intuitively understand the importance of developing talent, employee development often falls by the wayside. After all, you can have the best intentions in the world—but if you fail to put those intentions into action, they are meaningless. I find there are four main reasons why organizations fall short in developing the potential of their employees:

## #1: It is not today's issue.

Our plates are full every day. Just trying to get through the never-ending list of daily tasks seems like a pipe dream. Development is one of those highly critical issues that is easy to put off until next week. The problem with that approach is that next week never arrives. The only answer is to make development a priority. It is a large project, so break it up into smaller, manageable chunks. Construct a timeline for each specific step. Commit to reviewing progress on regular, pre-determined intervals. Talent development IS today's issue.

## #2: Success breeds complacency.

The most dangerous time for a company is often when things are going well. We are so busy with all the business we have cultivated, we don't feel the pressure to build for tomorrow. Oftentimes, companies wait until things turn downward before they wake up to the reality that employees arc becoming disgruntled, talent is leaving and there is no established pipeline of talent to take their place. At this point, it is too late for employee development.

## #3: They don't have the resources.

Talent development does require a commitment of resources. However, there are several lower cost tactics you can employ that will help people realize their potential. For instance, in-house mentoring and coaching are a good start. Create a book club and form some discussion groups. Webinars and virtual trainings are very cost effective. Don't let budget limitations deter you from building a powerful, effective development program for your team. After all, employee turnover will cost you far more in long run.

## #4: Fear of losing talent after investing in their development.

This one is particularly true for many small businesses. These business owners often tell me, "Why should I spend money on training when the employee is going to end up leaving?" As a small business person myself, I am sympathetic to concerns about costs and the bottom line. When I was a news director in the television industry, I worked in a fairly small market where the pay scale for news reporters and videographers was quite low. I knew that after a couple of years I was going to lose many of those outstanding young professionals. I took the approach that I wanted to do everything I could to help them develop their talents, including helping them find a new position when it came down to that. I realized several benefits from this approach: those employees were more enthusiastic and engaged while they worked for me; we tended to keep people a little longer than we would have if we didn't encourage their development; and we developed a reputation for helping professionals advance their careers, which helped us land high-quality entry-level talent.

## BUILD A PEOPLE FIRST CULTURE

The foundation of a great development program is your company culture. When you have a people first culture, your focus is on what is best for each team member, as opposed to what is best for you as the leader. Your success flows from their success. If each team member flourishes, the entire team benefits. People want to work in that kind of culture. People are attracted to that kind of culture. People will stay longer, be more productive and perform at their highest potential in a people first culture. A people first culture allows you to connect on a deeper level with each individual, which in turn allows you to better identify their potential and co-create strategies to help them develop that potential to the fullest.

Author John C. Maxwell writes of the importance of seeing the world from others' point of view. In *The Leader's Greatest Return* (HarperCollins Leadership 2020), Maxwell says he spent a lot of time in his career trying to persuade others to adopt his perspective—until he began to understand that wasn't an effective approach. (2)

> *"Slowly, I began to learn how others thought and to lead from where they are, not from where I was. While people's hopes and dreams may be unique, they share many characteristics, and as a leader, you can connect with them when you learn these things."—John C. Maxwell*

Here is what Maxwell learned:

- Most people are insecure. Give them confidence.
- Most people want to feel special. Compliment them.
- Most people want a bright future. Give them hope.
- Most people want to be understood. Listen to them.
- Most people want direction. Walk with them.
- Most people are selfish. Speak to their needs first.
- Most people get emotionally low. Encourage them.
- Most people want to be included. Ask their opinion.

- Most people want success. Help them win.
- Most people want to be appreciated. Give them credit. (3)

Understanding the perspective of others and where they are coming from not only allows you to lead them more effectively; it also increases trust between you and the team, which cultivates the kind of authentic leadership that builds loyalty.

## PUTTING DEVELOPMENT INTO ACTION

When Gallup completed a global study of the future of work, the organization revealed its findings in the book, *It's the Manager* (Gallup Press 2019) by Jim Clifton and Jim Harter. The authors identified four dominant patterns in organizations that have built a high-development culture:

### 1. The high-development cultures are CEO and board initiated.

To be effective, development has to come from the top. The highest executives must initiate the effort and map the strategy for improvement, including identifying where the organization is today and where it is headed in the future.

I would add one additional point here. I believe it is important for the top leaders of the organization to go first in whatever leadership initiative is put in place. If it is a coaching initiative, top executives should be the first ones to be coached. If it is training, the C-Suite folks should be among the first to be trained. I have conducted numerous trainings with emerging and high potential leaders who at some point of the training will say something like, "This is great, but why aren't our bosses going through this?"

I have had the privilege of teaching the Fit Leader's Program™ within the Michigan Department of Corrections for several years. The program was initiated by the department director, and every manager at the top of the organization, including the director, have gone through the program. This is one of those areas where if you are going to talk the talk, it's really important that you walk the walk.

## 2. High-development cultures educate managers on new ways of managing.

They focus training programs to encourage local leaders to collaborate with their teams to solve problems rather than having those solutions be dictated from the top. Engagement, performance and training are all aligned. Training is tailored to manager's capability.

## 3. High-development cultures practice companywide communication.

The best organizations have outstanding human resource teams that build systems and teach managers how to develop employees. They have "champions networks" that collect and disseminate best practices throughout the organization.

## 4. High-development cultures hold managers accountable.

The authors say "tolerance of mediocrity is the enemy of the best organizations." Amen. Amen. Amen! If leaders fail to hold managers accountable, that pretty much guarantees mediocrity across-the-board. When leaders are not held accountable, everyone notices. (4)

Here are a few more tips based on best practices I have seen across organizations with high-development cultures:

- **Develop a good onboarding program.** This is your opportunity to make a great first impression. A well-conceived onboarding program is the best way to "close the sale" and leave new team members feeling like they have chosen the right organization. Onboarding introduces them to growth opportunities, helps them understand how the organization functions and allows them to be aligned with where the team is headed. Use this experience to connect new employees to a mentor to help ensure their success.

- **Set annual goals and conduct quarterly reviews.** I am not a fan of performance reviews. On the other hand, I am a fan of every team member having written goals that are shared with the supervisor. Use the annual goals as an opportunity to co-create an action plan with each team member. Conduct quarterly or even monthly reviews and/or coaching sessions to monitor progress, identify barriers and make adjustments as needed. This is a great way to build in progress that excites the employee and holds them accountable for results.

- **Take a customized approach.** There is not a one-size-fits-all approach to developing human potential. Every person is unique in their talents, background, perspective and make-up. Therefore, your approach to developing them must play to those unique characteristics. Your approach will vary based on whether the employee is a low performer or high potential.

- **Offer a fair, effective compensation system.** Define what excellence looks like and reward it. When people fall short, be specific as to where those shortfalls occur and develop a plan to help them overcome the challenges. When everyone gets the same raise, it discourages innovation and creativity and breeds a disgruntled and unproductive workforce. Morale plummets, and so will your business.

- **Conduct exit interviews.** People do leave. Find out why. We interview people before they come to work for us. Do the same when they leave. There is a treasure trove of information available through the wisdom of departing employees. Tap into it and use that information to make your organization stronger.

- **Don't give answers. Ask questions.** It is easy for leaders to fall into the trap of providing answers to team members. It makes sense because leaders have risen to their position as a result of demonstrated excellence. People come to leaders looking for direction. So, we give it to them.

Yet instead of giving answers, consider the power of asking a question. What would you do? What do you think the best options might be? There is brain science behind this. When you give people a directive, their brains are in neutral—meaning they are not as engaged in the process. When you ask them a question, their brains are in gear. They are not only engaged; they are now more vested in the outcome because they own it.

Avoid using questions that start with "why," as those questions make people feel defensive and they might shut down. Instead, start questions with "what" or "how." Using open-ended questions will encourage people to talk and be more fully engaged in the discussion.

Asking questions also develops people's problem-solving and decision-making skills, which helps build their leadership abilities. There's another added benefit: Once those skills are more fully developed, they won't need to ask you as many questions because they will have confidence in their own abilities to make decisions and move forward. This not only builds a stronger, more engaged team; it also will free up your time to focus on other things that require your attention.

There are many different development approaches you can take depending on the employee and the nature of your organization. Encourage team members to network. (I would suggest a training on this one!) Encourage employees to add certifications and classroom experience with company financial support, if possible. Encourage them to join professional organizations and attend conferences.

Another approach that can spark your employees' desire to grow within the organization is cross-department training. This gives each employee a broader skill set and increases the versatility of your team. I worked with one organization that offers an internal coaching program where coaches work with coaches from other departments. This has resulted in many positive impacts for the company, including an increased understanding of different perspectives, stronger interdepartmental relationships and improved communication throughout the organization.

I recently had a coaching contract with an organization that offered a high-development culture. People truly enjoyed working there. A high percentage of employees remained with this company for their entire career. One employee I was coaching there told me, "I would walk to the end of the earth for this company because I know they would do the same for me."

Be a leader who sees potential in others—potential that even they don't know exists within themselves. Push them to go places they did not think they were capable of going. Be a leader with an unrelenting commitment to helping your team members identify and develop their potential to the fullest. If you are willing to go there for them, they will be willing to go to the end of the earth for you.

## COACHING TIPS

**Coaching Tip #1:** Identify the person or people who believed in your potential at some point in your life. What have they meant for your career?

**Coaching Tip #2:** Develop/review development plans with each of your team members. Schedule periodic reviews, at least quarterly.

# LEADERSHIP INSIGHT #11:

# Live Your Leadership Legacy Every Day

*"What counts in life is not the mere fact that we have lived.
It is what difference we have made to the lives of others that
will determine the significance of the life we lead."*
—*Nelson Mandela*

One of my family's favorite weekly activities is going out to breakfast after church. For many years, we have gathered at a favorite restaurant with dear friends to enjoy food and conversation together. Sharen has always loved every opportunity to be with people—but since the stroke has limited how often she can get out of the house, these weekly trips are something she really treasures. The restaurant staff caters to her every need, and in some respects, they have become like extended family. One day when I was paying the bill, I shared a story with the kitchen manager about how much Sharen works to overcome challenges with her disability. The kitchen manager offered this observation:

"She is a warrior."

Sharen has always had the ability to quickly make friends, and wherever we go, she is treated like a celebrity. After her shoulder replacement surgery, Sharen spent eight days in the hospital due to some complications. I remember texting a friend about how much the nurses loved Sharen. My friend's response:

"Everybody loves Sharen."

Sharen has always hated going on doctor's visits, and these days she has lots of doctors to see. One day as she was complaining about her next upcoming doctor's visit, our daughter pointed out how important it is for Sharen to stay on top of all her medical issues—in essence because the rest of the family needs her.

"You're the glue that holds the family together."

I often think of Sharen as an Angel that God has sent to be with me. I am incredibly blessed. Because of who she is, how she gives of herself to others and how much love she shows for life, Sharen has built a lasting legacy that makes an impact on family and friends daily.

A legacy is not about what you can achieve for yourself; it is about what you can do for others. It is about making a difference in as many lives as possible and leaving the world in a better place.

She is a warrior. Everybody loves Sharen. The glue that holds our family together. An Angel of God. That is Sharen's legacy crafted by how she has chosen to live her life, through good times and bad. It is a legacy worth celebrating.

## WHY LEADERS SHOULD CARE ABOUT THEIR LEGACY

You may feel you have more pressing issues to deal with today than worrying about what people are going to think about you after you ride off into the sunset. However, I would argue there is nothing more important to your leadership than your legacy. I believe there are three primary reasons why you should care about your leadership legacy:

**#1: As a legacy-leaver, you have the most potential to positively impact the lives of others.**

Legacy-leavers influence people daily, simply by who they are as leaders. You will make a lasting impact that will influence how others choose to live and lead. Most of the time, you will have no idea who you have impacted and the difference you have made in their lives.

One of my earliest legacy-leavers was my eighth-grade teacher and coach, Gary Williams. He was my first male school teacher and also the coach of our football and basketball teams. He was a tough yet compassionate leader who inspired us to learn and play hard. Our football team won all its games that year. I'll never forget his post-game speech after the final victory for the championship—it was made for the movies!

Mr. Williams was confined to a wheelchair. Living a somewhat sheltered, small-town life, it was my first exposure to an individual dealing with disabilities. Because his home was on my paper route, I had the opportunity to see how he lived and the ramp to his front door. He was paralyzed below the waist, but he was able to drive. I remember how impressed I was at his upper body strength, most evidenced by his ability to easily shoot free throws from his wheelchair. (Give it a try sometime.)

Despite his physical challenges, Mr. Williams never lost his competitive spirit. He played on a highly competitive wheelchair basketball team. He instilled that same competitive zeal in the players he coached. He went on in life to become the athletic director for another public school district. In the classroom, Gary Williams' job was to teach his students English and history. As a coach, he taught the basics of football and basketball. As a leader, he left a legacy: how to refuse to let challenges defeat you in life, how to work as a team to achieve your goals, and how to encourage and inspire others.

It may not have been Mr. Williams' intention, but the way he led his life left a lasting impression on me and no doubt many others. As best-selling authors James Kouzes and Barry Posner note in their book, *A Leader's Legacy* (John Wiley & Sons, Inc. 2006) (1), legacy leaders commit themselves to making a difference:

> *"By asking ourselves how we want to be remembered, we plant seeds for living our lives as if we matter. By living each day as if we matter, we offer up our own unique legacy. By offering up our own unique legacy, we make the world we inhabit a better place than we found it."*
> —*James M. Kouzes & Barry Z. Posner*

## #2: Your legacy represents the potential to do good in your community.

During tough times, it is easy to retrench and focus on your own survival. Legacy thinkers never lose sight of the greater good. The COVID-19 pandemic in 2020 represented an unprecedented challenge for the world. In addition to the human suffering, the lockdowns enforced in many states caused immense financial challenges for individual employees who were laid off as well as businesses that saw their operations curtailed and shutdown.

The challenges associated with working remotely brought unique stress to families across the country, especially those with young children and elderly loved ones. In addition to serious health concerns brought about by the coronavirus, mental health issues during and after the crisis were prevalent. First responders and healthcare workers were overwhelmed by the avalanche of needs thrust upon their systems.

I was simply amazed at the outpouring of goodwill that occurred during the COVID-19 pandemic. In every community across the country, people seemed to set aside their own concerns to rise up and lend support where it was needed. Citizens delivered food to healthcare workers and offered moral support through organized demonstrations of appreciation. Police officers delivered groceries and medicine to the elderly. Businesses large and small, most of them suffering severe economic fallout from the crisis, used their expertise to provide equipment and supplies needed in their communities and across the country. Manufacturers retooled their plants and called back laid off workers to build ventilators and other personal protective equipment. Many organizations donated masks, face shields and gloves or started fundraisers. Financial support poured in to aid the non-profit network as food banks and other organizations struggled to keep up with needs in their community.

No one wanted the COVID-19 crisis to happen. When it did, legacy thinkers emerged to make a difference in their communities. Our world is a better place because so many people were eager to rise above the lousy hand we were dealt and support people who needed it most.

### #3: Your legacy allows the potential to benefit future generations.

The Lansing, Michigan area has benefitted from the legacy of a businessman by the name of R.E. Olds. In the early part of the 20th century, R.E. Olds moved his fledging automotive company to Lansing. The result has been automotive history.

For more than a century, General Motors has built vehicles in Lansing, and generations of families have worked at the GM plants there. Prosperity reigned as grandparents, parents and children worked and made a good life for their families as a result of their GM employment. The presence of the world's largest automaker led to the creation of thousands of other businesses that provided jobs, built neighborhoods, schools and parks. The quality of life enjoyed by tens of thousands allowed for community support of a non-profit network that provided services to the less fortunate in the community. Despite the ebb and flow of an auto-based economy, the Lansing region has enjoyed the fruits of the GM legacy.

In the late 1990s a General Motors executive paid a visit to then Lansing Mayor David Hollister. The news was not good. Oldsmobile as a brand was fading. After the current line-up of vehicles being manufactured in Lansing was finished with its scheduled production in a few years, there were no future models planned for Lansing's GM facilities. Suddenly, after a century-long love affair, Lansing was staring in the face of a total shutdown of General Motors operations.

Needless to say, the situation was bleak. Not only was Lansing going to lose all the GM employment—but the GM spin-off effect that had been so positive for decades was now going to turn in the other direction.

The situation may have appeared hopeless to most, but Mayor Hollister and a number of other business and community leaders simply refused to give up. A concerted effort began to convince GM to continue operations in Lansing. The odds were long, some said impossible. To make the situation even more complicated, the Keep GM effort was attempting get people who didn't always work well together to support a common cause. The Lansing region had a well-deserved reputation of being very parochial – political leaders who would not work together because of a desire to serve their own self interests. It was not a recipe for success.

There were numerous obstacles along the way. Mayor Hollister and other city leaders were most interested in keeping GM physically located in the city of Lansing. Suburban leaders thought a new, state-of-the-art facility outside the city was the best approach. Leaders at both the local and state level had to be convinced to support a complex package of tax incentives to pull the entire deal together. The United Auto Workers had to sign off on allowing for robots inside the manufacturing operations, which would lead to a consolidation of the number of jobs in the region.

In the end, everyone rose up for the common good. Suburban leaders signed off on supporting the urban location. The UAW recognized that keeping some jobs was better than no jobs. The tax incentive package came together. The result: General Motors ended up spending billions to retool the existing urban plant AND build a new plant in the suburbs. Since the early 2000s, GM has continued to build some of its best-selling models in its line-up at manufacturing facilities now recognized as among the finest in the world.

The work of the Keep GM group saved what looked like a lost cause and kept GM in the region. Thousands of other jobs related to nearby auto suppliers serving GM have also been introduced into the area. People were willing to set aside their own personal interests and make some real sacrifices to provide an opportunity for a better life for the entire region. The results are still felt today and will continue to be realized for many years to come.

## CONNECTING TO YOUR "WHY"

Why do you do what you do?

Defining and living your legacy will connect you to a powerful "why" that will cause you to be more engaged—and as others embrace your vision, this will result in higher levels of engagement on your team. Higher engagement equals higher productivity and better results.

Being excited about why we do what we do gets everyone enthused about coming to work. The "why" represents their opportunity to leave a lasting impact on the world.

Steve Jobs, who is widely viewed as the father of the personal computer, co-founded Apple in 1976. He was forced out of Apple in a power struggle in 1985. He went on to form another company and returned to a struggling Apple in 1997. The products Apple developed under his leadership (iPod, iPad, iTunes, iPhone, etc.) revolutionized the world. Under Jobs' leadership, Apple was listed by Forbes as the "Most Admired Company" in the world.

Apple excelled during Jobs' tenure in all the key metrics: it became the second largest music retailer behind Walmart and number one among Fortune 500 companies when it came to shareholder returns. At one time, Jobs was estimated to be worth between $6.5 and $7 billion. Those are the kind of numbers that make a CEO loved far and wide. However, when reflecting on that success, Jobs talked about what really motivated him:

*"Being the richest man in the cemetery doesn't matter to me. Going to bed at night saying we've done something wonderful, that's what matters to me."—Steve Jobs*

Steve Jobs was a man connected to his "why." He had the right vision for his life and his company. That was reflected in the bottom-line results. There is ample research that shows that organizations that are connected to a vision or a higher calling have greater profits than those that are simply in business to make money. (2)

On December 1, 1955, Rosa Parks refused when a bus driver demanded that she give up her seat in the "colored section" for a white passenger after the "white section" filled up. She was arrested for civil disobedience for violating Alabama's segregation laws. Her willingness to serve as a leader in the first major civil rights campaign of the postwar era inspired blacks throughout Montgomery, Alabama to boycott the bus system. The protest triggered a federal lawsuit that successfully ended segregation on public buses in Montgomery.

Rosa Parks' bold actions did not come without costs. She endured death threats for years and was fired from her job as a seamstress in a local department store. She eventually moved to Detroit and worked for Congressman John Conyers.

Rosa Parks' "why" was, in her own words, being "tired of giving in" and a steadfast commitment to the civil rights movement. Known as the "first lady of the civil rights movement," Rosa Parks was the first woman to lie in honor in the Capitol Rotunda. Her legacy started with a simple refusal to give up her seat on the bus. Her lasting impact is still felt generations later. (3)

Susan B. Anthony was born into a family committed to social justice. As a teen, she was actively involved in collecting anti-slavery petitions. She became a leading advocate for women's rights and African Americans. She engaged in civil disobedience by voting in her hometown. This resulted in a court case in which she was convicted and ordered to pay a fine, which she refused to do. During her years of tirelessly campaigning for women's suffrage, she was accused of trying to destroy the institution of marriage. Anthony and her colleague, Elizabeth Stanton developed and presented to Congress a proposed constitutional amendment giving women the right to vote. The amendment became known as the Susan B. Anthony Amendment and eventually became the 19th Amendment to the U.S. Constitution. (4)

Steve Jobs, Rosa Parks and Susan B. Anthony left powerful legacies that have impacted the lives of people around the world. They were people who were clearly connected to their "why." They did not pursue their dreams for personal benefit, but chose to build a legacy by making the world a better place. Their visions were widely embraced by those who shared their dream. If you wish to be a legacy-leaver, develop a "why" that will cause others to be excited to be part of the team. Ultimately, this will make your "why" a reality.

## CREATE YOUR LEGACY STATEMENT

I encourage all leaders to develop an individual legacy statement. This statement defines who you are as a leader. It should inspire you and clearly communicate how you want to be viewed by your team and other stakeholders. I ask many of my clients to develop a legacy statement, which serves as a basis for much of our coaching. Many of my clients have framed their legacy statement and hung it on the wall in their office.

As you begin to ponder your legacy statement, think about what you want to accomplish. This is your opportunity to reflect and ask yourself some deep questions. Do you desire to leave the world a better place when you are finished? What does that look like?

As you go through this process, ask yourself the most powerful coaching question of all: What else? Be prepared to let this process play out for a few days before sitting down to actually draft your statement.

Legacies come in all shapes and sizes. You are unique, and your legacy statement should be the same. Some people advocate a one or two-sentence legacy statement. Others like taking a more expansive approach with a series of statements that encapsulate their leadership "why."

To give you an example, here is my legacy statement:

**As a leader, I will live my values every day.** My values are the foundation on which I stand and the key to unlocking my full potential as a leader. They influence every decision I make and every step I take.

**As a leader, I will demonstrate empathy towards others.** I will respect different viewpoints and different sets of experiences. I will seek to connect to the emotions that others are experiencing.

**As a leader, I will seek to help develop the full potential of every team member.** I will help others see potential in themselves. I will co-create and implement a growth plan for each team member.

**As a leader, I will invest myself into others.** I will let each team member know that I believe in them by listening, affirming, mentoring, challenging and holding them accountable.

**As a leader, I will commit myself to positivity.** I refuse to allow negative forces overcome me and dominate my thinking. I recognize that positivity allows people to overcome barriers and inspire others.

**As a leader, I will seek to encourage others in their career.** I will be their cheerleader, praise their strengths and acknowledge their accomplishments. I will deliver authentic compliments.

**As a leader, I will demonstrate humility.** It is not about me. It is about those I lead. I will put the goals and needs of others before my own.

**As a leader, if I am not teaching, I will be learning.** The key to transformation is continuous learning. The farther I travel down the road of my leadership journey, the more I realize how much more I must learn.

**As a leader, I will demonstrate resilience in the face of every challenge.** I will adjust and adapt to misfortunes and setbacks. I will view challenges as an opportunity for growth.

The value of hanging your legacy statement in plain sight is that you can challenge yourself every day on whether you are living out your legacy. It should also communicate who you are as a leader to everyone who sees that statement. It will inspire others and allow them to hold you accountable for how you want to be viewed.

## LIVE YOUR LEGACY

One of the keys to effectively living your legacy is the vision and willingness to take the long view while continuing to focus on your day-to-day work as a leader. This can be particularly challenging because most people around you will be focused on the here and now. This includes your direct reports, peers and your boss. We understandably have to focus on making our numbers today. If we don't do that successfully, we won't be around tomorrow!

During my years in television, I worked for a public company. One of the first things I learned about life in the public lane is everything is broken down into 90-day cycles. Numbers are reported to Wall Street every three months. As leaders we had to be fixated on making our bottom line every 90 days. Life became a set of numbers on a profit and loss statement or balance sheet. In that environment, it was easy to lose sight of the people behind the numbers and the purpose behind why we existed. Oftentimes with public companies, the long view ceases to exist and the legacy can be lost.

Walt Disney was a pioneer in cartoon production, animation, film and television. He holds the record for the most Academy Awards. In the 1950s, Disney expanded his growing empire into the amusement park arena when he opened Disneyland in Anaheim, California. Once he moved into the amusement park industry, Disney chose to focus much of his personal time in that area. His vision was to create clean parks that provided the best in family fun.

Disneyland was an enormous success, as was just about everything in which Walt Disney chose to be involved. Not one to rest on his incredible accomplishments, Disney announced a new vision in the mid-1960s: the creation of Disney World near Orlando, Florida. Disney World would not only include an expanded version of the popular Magic Kingdom, it also would feature golf courses, resort hotels and a new amusement park focused on the future – EPCOT Center.

Walt Disney died in 1966 before his vision of Disney World came to fruition. However, his leadership legacy that he lived every day flourished after he passed away. His team enthusiastically embraced and executed the Disney World project. Decades later, following enormous growth including more theme parks and the latest in entertainment, Disney's mission remains intact. As Walt Disney laid out in his initial vision more than six decades earlier, all Disney properties are committed to cleanliness and the best in customer satisfaction. Employees are empowered to do whatever they feel is necessary to ensure their customers are happy with the Disney experience. That is a big part of Walt Disney's legacy. (5)

## SEIZE YOUR MOMENTS OF COURAGE

On October 9, 2012, Malala Yousafzai and two of her friends were shot by a Taliban gunman while riding a bus in her native Pakistan. The assassination attempt was made due to Malala's courageous work as an activist for female education and as a human rights advocate. Though she was shot in the head and rendered unconscious, she eventually recovered from her wounds. There was an international outpouring of condemnation for the attacks—so much so that Muslim clerics in Pakistan condemned the attacks.

Following her recovery, Malala became an international leader in the right for education. She founded a non-profit organization, co-authored an international best seller and became the youngest Nobel Prize laureate. At the young age of 16, she spoke to the United Nations for worldwide access for education, an event dubbed "Malala Day." She received several standing ovations. Among her words that day:

*"The terrorists thought they would change my aims and stop my ambitions, but nothing changed in my life except this: weakness, fear and hopelessness died. Strength, power and courage was born ... I am not against anyone,*

*neither am I here to speak in terms of personal revenge against the Taliban or any other terrorist group. I'm here to speak up for the right of education for every child. I want education for the sons and daughters of the Taliban and all terrorists and extremists." (6)—Malala Yousafzai*

Malala seized her moment of courage and is leaving a legacy of hope, strength and courage that continues to spread across the globe. She is an inspiration!

You don't always know when your moment for courage will come in your life. For me, it was after Sharen suffered her stroke. As a family, we were forced to head down a path we couldn't see towards a destination where we had never been. We had to set aside selfishness, fear and a comfortable life. In their place came greater love, a stronger relationship with God, determination and a level of joy we had never known before.

In their research, Kouzes and Posner found that every person they interviewed has a story about courage in their lives. In most cases, those stories of courage involved every day encounters with life. Some stories were about mundane things. People told of conquering stage fright, getting outside their comfort zone, feeling lost physically or spiritually, quitting jobs or going back to school. Among their conclusions, the authors say that courage is what they called the "X factor" in change. (7).

*"Leadership is about taking people to the places they've never been before, and we can't go to those places without courage. Leadership is courage in action. Courage gives us the energy to move forward. Courage gives us the confidence to believe we can make it. Courage gives us the strength to sustain ourselves in our darkest hours.*

*Courage enables us to leave a legacy that declares, 'I was here and I made a difference.'"—James M. Kouzes &
Barry Z. Posner*

Most recently, the COVID-19 pandemic provided ample opportunities for moments of courage for many of us as leaders. We had to confront new realities and manage the fears of those around us as we reentered the workplace filled with doubt and uncertainty. Business models had to be changed. Many businesses closed their doors. The "new normal" as it was called required new thinking, new vision, new levels of cooperation and collaboration, and renewed determination to overcome new barriers placed in front of us.

Are you ready to seize your next moment of courage? If so, you will be able to say you were there and you made a difference!

## COACHING TIPS

**Coaching Tip #1:** Ask your team to consider why they do what they do. Are they connected to their "why"? How do your team members want to make the world a better place.?

**Coaching Tip #2:** Reflect on the moments of courage in your life. What patterns do you notice? What changed as a result? How will you better prepare yourself for the next moment of courage?

# LEADERSHIP INSIGHT #12:

# Chart Your Journey on Transformation Highway

*"Transformational leaders don't start by denying the world around them. Instead, they describe a future they'd like to create."—Seth Godin*

Caregiving has had an enormous transformational impact on my life. I am not the same person or the same leader I was before Sharen suffered her stroke. Of course, I would hope that the combination of life experience, maturity and wisdom also caused a great deal of change in me over the years. However, there is no doubt that being a caregiver has been responsible for major shifts in how I look at the world, how I relate to others and how I respond to daily events.

For much of my life, I centered my thinking around me. I was, frankly, pretty selfish. I have also been guilty of lacking patience, humility, empathy and loving myself more than others. I have been guilty of not appreciating what I already have in life, often focusing on what I did not have. While I was making a bit of progress in many of those areas in the years leading up to Sharen's stroke, when I was thrust into the role of caregiver, it dramatically changed my outlook, attitude and the lens through which I view the world.

Being a caregiver caused me to put Sharen's needs before my own, to think of myself less and to view the world from her perspective rather than mine. Things that were important to her became important to me. For Sharen, it has always been of the highest importance to do things for me. As her caregiver, I soon found that doing things for her became important to me.

Of course, there have been challenges. There were many times when I would tire, especially towards the end of the weekend, and I would react badly. What I soon came to understand was that in most instances, my reaction really wasn't due to the fact that Sharen had done anything wrong, but was more because I was feeling inconvenienced.

I prayed daily for patience, which slowly began to grow inside. There were days when Sharen told me I had the patience of Job and others when she angrily told me I had a lot of work to do in that area. Frankly, both were true. I have learned over the years that transformation doesn't occur overnight. It is a process that requires steady, determined commitment to change.

After a while, the changes in my personal life began to show up in my professional life. Things that used to make me angry became insignificant or I began to view those issues through the prism of other people. In my coaching and training relationships, it became incredibly important to focus on the agenda of other people and tap into my growing ability to empathize. I also found myself more willing to be vulnerable with clients. When I shared some of my failings in life, clients struggling with the same issues found comfort in the fact that they were not alone and there was hope in making positive change going forward.

Today, you are not the leader you were ten years ago, five years ago or even one year ago. Change, which is occurring at the fastest pace in history, mandates that you continually evolve and grow. If you do not constantly evolve, you will be left behind. Not only is transformation critically important for you personally, but it's also essential for your professional life. Your team needs you to lead them into a new era with new ideas and a fresh perspective. Transformational leaders have the power to inspire and motivate the team and build a culture where innovation flourishes. You will be challenged, sometimes daily, to initiate, sell and manage change initiatives. Transformational leaders will develop transformational teams that results in transformational organizations.

Are you willing to be that leader?

## TRANSFORMATION HIGHWAY IS FILLED WITH POTHOLES

The process of transformation is a journey that takes place over your entire lifetime. Once we start this journey, we travel along a road—I call it Transformation Highway—to our final destination. The roadway is not always smooth. In fact, Transformation Highway is filled with potholes. (I live in Michigan, so I know a thing or two about potholes!) There are lots of winding curves and more than a few detours along the way. The journey is often stressful, causing us to shout a few unpleasantries to other drivers along the way. The journey is often tiring and drains our energy. Those challenges can have a negative impact on how we view life, affecting our own personality and the view of those around us. We also can choose to focus on the beauty that is around us every day, whether it is the people who are travelling with us, the scenery, the excitement of experiencing new things and different people, or the anticipation of reaching our ultimate destination.

Your growth as a leader is constantly evolving. Your journey will be challenging—daily. You will have disappointments and failures along the way. You will feel stuck on a plateau for months at a time, frustrated by your inability to move forward. You will worry about finances, competition, constant change, workforce challenges, your family and friends and forces in the world that you can't begin to control. You can choose to allow these circumstances to negatively impact your development as a leader. Or, you can choose to learn from each challenge you face and use that learning experience as a growth opportunity.

Along the way, you are going to encounter amazing people who make work and life worthwhile. You will be inspired, mentored, motivated, affirmed, encouraged, prayed over, challenged, held accountable, lifted up, strengthened and comforted. You, in turn, can use those character-shaping moments in your life to not only fuel your growth as a leader, but also to be that leader for everyone else in your world. You choose!

Eleanor Roosevelt was the longest serving First Lady in U.S. history, working alongside her husband Franklin D. Roosevelt during his four terms in office. FDR's successor Harry Truman called her the "First Lady of the World." As a human rights activist, Eleanor was opinionated and controversial and spoke out on behalf of civil rights for African Americans—not a universally popular concept in the 1940s.

Life's journey was challenging in many aspects and could have easily derailed Eleanor Roosevelt at numerous points in her life. She lost both parents and one of her brothers at a young age. She was devastated upon learning of her husband's affair with another woman, yet chose to stay married and find her role as an activist in the world. When her husband suffered a debilitating paralysis that cost him the use of both legs, she encouraged him to remain in public office. After FDR's disability, she began making speeches, public appearances and press conferences on her own. Among her notable accomplishments was serving as the U.S. delegate to the United Nations.

Eleanor Roosevelt's character was shaped by forces and obstacles that would have destroyed many human beings. Her decisions on how to respond to those forces had a transformational impact on her life and the world. Widely recognized as one of the most esteemed people in the world, Eleanor Roosevelt was included on Gallup's list of the Most Widely Admired People of the 20th Century. (1)

Andrew Carnegie became one of the richest men in history as a result of his leadership in building the American steel industry in the 19th century. He also became the world's leading philanthropist, giving away about 90 percent of his fortune—$350 million—in the final years of his life. Among his most noteworthy endeavors was his leadership role in the creation of the public library system in the United States.

Carnegie's work ethic was largely shaped as a result of growing up in a poor family in Scotland. When his father's work as a hand weaver fell on hard times and the country was afflicted by starvation, the family decided to move to Allegheny, Pennsylvania. Carnegie and his father both took jobs in a cotton mill, starting at $1.20 per week. His father later quit, leaving Andrew as the main breadwinner for the family. Through the years, his business acumen led to numerous successes and resulted in him becoming quite wealthy.

Carnegie's transformation in life led him to focus on philanthropic activities. He believed those of great wealth had a responsibility to use that wealth for the greater good. He devoted the rest of his life to the advancement of social and educational causes. His wealth led to the creation of 3,000 libraries across the country. Though libraries have changed a great deal, particularly in this digital age, the mission remains the same—distributing information to the masses. (2)

The journey down Transformation Highway will take you in many directions. Make sure you enjoy the journey, especially the potholes and detours, and even the lousy drivers you encounter along the way. How you choose to respond, learn and grow from these challenges can have a transformational impact on the world. Seize the opportunity and make a difference in your life and the lives of those around you.

## CONTINUOUS LEARNING FOSTERS TRANSFORMATION

If you hope to keep up with rapidly changing trends, competitive forces, technology and workforce issues, continuous learning is vital. Continuous learning is the essential ingredient that fosters long-term transformation in your leadership. You need the latest information to make decisions and tackle complex problem-solving in today's world. Most important of all, transformation brought on by continuous learning is crucial in your ability to relate to an increasingly diverse and ever-changing talent pool—particularly in this era when we have four generations with drastically different life influences affecting our thinking, expectations, priorities and world views.

Florence Nightingale, known as the Lady of the Lamp for her work with wounded soldiers, is credited as the founder of modern nursing. As a social activist, she worked to improve healthcare for all in British society and advocated for hunger relief in India. She wrote extensively to share her medical knowledge with the world. She was a leader in creating infographics to help explain complex medical information to the masses. Florence Nightingale was a life-long learner, from her early childhood days and all throughout adulthood. During her travels around the world, she eagerly shared her extensive knowledge with others. Her commitment to nursing and continuous learning was evidenced by the creation of the first secular nursing school in the world, based in London. Her transformation undoubtedly influenced the growth of nurses and the nursing profession well beyond her lifetime. (3)

You can engage in continuous learning at anytime, anywhere and in any fashion that suits you best. When it comes to continuous learning, there is no one-size-fits-all approach. What matters most is your desire to learn, grow and be transformed. You certainly should take advantage of any high-quality trainings made available to you through your organization. There are numerous other approaches to continuing education that will vary depending on your current situation. Reading, listening to podcasts and attending webinars are great low cost or no cost ways to learn, and you can easily fit them into your busy lifestyle. Thanks to technology, it's easier and more convenient than ever to earn degrees and certifications. In today's world, there is really no excuse for not learning, and there is no stage in your career when you can't learn and grow.

It is also a good idea to have a vision of where you want to head in your career. That vision can serve as a blueprint to encourage you to achieve your goals. Oftentimes in coaching, I have my clients complete a five-year vision plan to help focus their thinking. In crafting such a plan, it helps to think about the end goal. Develop a picture in your mind of where you would like to be in five years. In thinking about what that picture looks like, consider each year in the five-year plan and what specific steps you want to take to reach your specified goal.

For example, if you would like a promotion at work and feel an advanced degree is necessary to receive that promotion, think about when and how you will pursue that degree. Build a timeline to hold yourself accountable.

Of course, things will change along the way. There is no such thing as a five-year plan that is cast in stone. Life happens. You will have to be flexible, but a vision plan will get you excited about future possibilities and energize you to take action in your life.

As you work on your own commitment to growth, you should also build a continuous learning culture on your team. There are plenty of bottom-line reasons why continuous learning makes good business sense: organizations with continuous learning cultures enjoy higher productivity and greater innovation. Most importantly, when leaders create the mindset that continuous learning is an expectation and open to all, team members flourish individually. They will be more engaged and much more likely to stay and grow with the organization.

## TRANSFORMATION OVER THE NEXT DECADE

Organizational culture has shifted dramatically during my career. Forty years ago, leadership was very much a top-down relationship. The generals gave the orders, and the troops went out and implemented. In the past two decades, there has been a shift to more of a coaching culture that features a collaborative approach to decision making. In this environment, effective leaders seek out diverse opinions, listen more than they talk, ask questions more than they give answers, promote a culture of consistent two-way feedback, and empower team members to do their jobs without constant oversight.

The breakneck pace of change in our global economy has never been more constant—a trend that will likely continue over the next decade. As a leader, you simply cannot afford to stand still in the years ahead or you will be left behind. I think Hall of Fame hockey star Wayne Gretzky summed it up pretty well:

> *"I skate to where the puck is going to be, not to where it has been."*—Wayne Gretzky

While many of the current organizational culture trends will likely continue, we can assume there will be major shifts in the next decade that will challenge us as leaders. We need to skate to where the puck is going to be. That means we must be thoughtful about emerging trends and consider how they will impact the skills we need and the development steps we should take to lead in the new environment.

In *The Future Leader* (Wiley 2020), author Jacob Morgan details nine skills and mindsets that leaders need to succeed in the next decade. According to Morgan, a variety of trends will influence leaders in the years ahead, including artificial intelligence, the pace of change, new talent landscape, purpose and meaning, morality, ethics, transparency and globalization. He says future leaders will need the essential skills to serve as a coach, futurist, technology teenager, translator and Yoda. Current research suggests leaders are not doing a well enough in those areas, he notes, which reveals the need for an additional mindset and skill for leaders in the future-optimism. (4).

> *"As a leader you have to wake up each day believing that the future can be better than it is today and that you can help build a better future."*—Jacob Morgan

One of the more forward-looking leaders of the generation was Herb Kelleher, co-founder of Southwest Airlines. Kelleher and his partner came up with the concept of a low-cost airline, an idea originally put into place by Pacific Southwest Airlines. Kelleher's approach was quite different than the norm for airlines. Southwest avoided the traditional hub-and-spoke model popular across the industry in favor of point-to-point service. The airline made low fares possible in part by abandoning some services offered by other airlines. As a result, passengers flocked to Southwest.

Not only was Kelleher a visionary when it came to the type of airline Southwest would become, but he also was forward-thinking in building an offbeat culture within the organization. Southwest received great notoriety for creating the type of unique office setting that Google and others in Silicon Valley became noted for decades later. Featuring a more casual atmosphere, the Southwest office boasted plenty of fun activities and management that didn't take themselves so seriously all the time. This made Southwest a highly desirable workplace destination for top talent. (5)

## TRANSFORM THE WORLD ONE LEADER AT A TIME

Our world is constantly shifting—which means leaders also must continually shift how they view the world, organizational culture, our communities, families and each other. As author Marshall Goldsmith points out (which also happens to be the title of his book), "What Got You Here Won't Get You There" (Hachette Books 2007). No matter how successful you have been, you can't be the same leader tomorrow that you were yesterday because it just won't work any longer. As the pace of change is constantly accelerating, leaders must evolve and grow or they and their teams will get left behind.

The times we live in are unlike any we have seen before. In the past months, we have been forced to rethink how we live, work and play as the result of a global pandemic. We have witnessed the pain of racial injustice that preys upon our country like a cancer. This is all happening against a backdrop of rising anger, fear and hatred that divides our country. There has been a loss of civility in how we communicate with each other and an increasing lack of tolerance for people who think, act and look differently than we do. This polarization is creating gulfs that seem impossible to bridge.

I believe there is a path forward to better times. That path must be blazed by leaders in business, education, government, healthcare, non-profits, communities and, most importantly, our families. We need leadership at all levels of society to lift up our country and carry us to a better place.

Our world desperately needs leaders who can embrace and celebrate differences, encourage multiple points of view, challenge the status quo and push the envelope on innovative approaches to problems. We need leaders who can unify where divisions exist, collaborate when communication breaks down, and find common ground to create solutions that others say cannot be achieved. We need leaders who will work tirelessly to break down barriers between people, work past historical divides that have separated us, and heal wounds that have festered far too long.

I realize we can't attain world peace or bridge the racial divide overnight. However, we have to start somewhere. What is our alternative?

My challenge to you is to be the type of leader the world needs. Resolve to change the world one person and one day at a time. Join with other like-minded leaders to build a better organization and a better community. As you start to achieve more success, others will notice. They will like what they see and join you. That is how it spreads. You can make a difference by modeling the behavior you want to see in others. Don't leave this to others. Make a decision to take charge to the best of your ability in your everyday world.

## THE TRANSFORMATION JOURNEY
## REQUIRES DAILY FOCUS

I recently took some time to reflect back on the leaders I have cited throughout this book. They are amazing group: Abraham Lincoln, Mahatma Gandhi, Jesus, Mother Teresa, John F. Kennedy, Apostle Paul, Martin Luther King Jr., Winston Churchill, Steve Jobs, Rosa Parks, Susan B. Anthony, Walt Disney, Malala Yousafzai, Eleanor Roosevelt, Andrew Carnegie, Florence Nightingale and Herb Kelleher. These incredible individuals tell the story of great leadership far better than I am capable of doing. They are diverse in their backgrounds, gender, race, color, socio-economic status, the era in which they lived, geography, religion, political views and the challenges they faced. I would not expect you to necessarily agree with every one of these leaders about any number of issues. Yet their status as great leaders is indisputable.

As diverse as they are, these great leaders have many things in common, including vision, being ahead of their time, determination, conviction and the ability to rally masses of people to support their cause. They all failed numerous times. They were harshly criticized, often threatened and suffered for their cause in ways that would have derailed the efforts of most others.

As I reflected on their work in relation to this book, something occurred to me: While I cited most of these leaders in just one chapter, each of them could have been cited as an example in every chapter of this book. For the most part, every one of these leaders lived all of the principles in this book, which underscores the fact that they were truly remarkable leaders.

You too have the ability to be a remarkable leader. Your lifetime journey along the road of transformation requires a daily focus on being a leader who inspires, motivates, engages, empowers, encourages, affirms, challenges, mentors and coaches, and holds yourself and others accountable.

You will fail. You will make mistakes. You will stumble and fall. You will be discouraged, anxious, fearful, stressed out, exhausted, angry, worried and confused. You also have the ability to persevere and overcome all of these obstacles. You can rise above the challenges, beat the odds and scale mountains that seem impossible to climb. You can accomplish your goals, live out your dreams and make a real difference in the lives of others along the way.

Envision the picture of who you would like to be as a leader and how you wish to be viewed. This picture *will* become reality if you strive to live out the insights discussed in this book to the best of your ability. Don't try to do everything at once. Focus on specific areas where you feel you have the best opportunity in the moment to thrive and grow.

For any team, the most important ingredient to success is leadership. It doesn't matter what industry sector, what size or where you live. Leadership is the driver of success or failure. This world needs great leaders. Now more than ever. Your work as a leader matters. Your contributions are valued, more than you know. Your potential for continued growth, if you are willing to cultivate it, is vast and exciting.

My prayer is that you will become the leader you were born to be. My hope is the world will experience the full measure of your leadership capability. My desire is for you to have a leadership life that leaves you fulfilled and satisfied with the knowledge that you have made a difference by leading to lift up others.

Enjoy the journey!

## COACHING TIPS

**Coaching Tip #1:** Encourage your team members to complete a five-year plan. Use the plan as a basis for several coaching conversations. Work with them develop strategies to help them achieve their vision for their own lives.

**Coaching Tip #2:** Review each of the leadership insights presented throughout this book. Score yourself on a 1-10 scale for where you feel you stand right now. Pick one behavior you feel represents the best current opportunity for you to grow as a leader. What specific things can you do in the next 90 days to improve your score by 1 or 2 points?

# SHOCKING STATISTICS
# ABOUT CAREGIVING

According to AARP, more than 1 in 5 Americans are caregivers, having provided care to an adult or child with special needs at some time in the past 12 months. That's a total of 53 million caregivers in the United States, an increase from 43.5 million from 2015. (1)

These numbers are based on a 2020 report entitled, *Caregiving in the U.S.*, presented by AARP and The National Alliance for Caregiving. The report attributes much of the spike in caregiving to three factors: an increasing number of aging baby boomers requiring care; limitations or workplace shortages in healthcare and long-term services; and increased efforts by states to facilitate home and community-based services. (2)

Other key findings include:

- Nearly one in five caregivers (19%) are providing unpaid care to an adult with health or functional needs.
- More Americans (24%) are caring for more than one person, up from 18% in 2015.
- More family caregivers (26%) have difficulty coordinating care, up from 19% in 2015.
- More Americans (26%) are caring for someone with Alzheimer's disease or dementia, up from 22% in 2015.
- More Americans (23%) say caregiving has made their own health worse, up from 17% in 2015.

- Family caregiving spans across all generations, including Boomers, Gen-X, Gen-Z, Millennials and Silent.
- 61% of family caregivers are also working. (3)

According to the report, most people say that caregiving has given them a sense of purpose or meaning. However, those feelings are mixed with increased stress, and many report that caregiving has negatively impacted their own health. (4)

The economic effect of family caregiving is substantial. One in 5 caregivers report high financial strain as a result of caregiving. Many caregivers report using up their short-term and long-term savings. More than half (60%) report that they are working while caregiving, and the majority of those caregivers report at least one work-related impact. One in 10 had to give up working altogether. (5)

In a separate AARP study on the financial impact of caregiving, researchers surveyed 2,000 family caregivers and asked them to keep a diary of their expenses. The study showed family caregivers spend an average of nearly $7,000 a year of their own money. Caregivers also report cutting back on many things because of the costs of caregiving, including trips or vacations (45%); eating out (45%); personal doctor visits (19%) and groceries (18%). (6)

Among the conclusions in the 2020 *Caregiving in the U.S.* report:

*"Unpaid Caregiving is increasing in prevalence and the U.S. population continues to age and live longer with more complex and chronic conditions. Caregivers feel the push and pull of providing care on their time, their financial well-being, their health, their family, their work, and their own personal well-being." (7)*

The report also concludes that as more people need care, there will be fewer people available to provide that care for them. The report states: "Without greater explicit support for family caregivers in coordination among the public and private sectors and across multiple disciplines, overall care responsibilities will likely intensify and place greater pressures on individuals within families, especially as baby boomers move into old age." (8)

As a society, we need to step up and address what I believe is a looming crisis in our country. We need to be able to responsibly and lovingly provide care for those who need it and offer a stronger network of support services and financial help for those called to the role of family caregiver.

Caregiving is, without question, the most rewarding thing I have ever done in my life. I have been blessed to have a loving, understanding, patient and abundantly positive wife who makes my work a joy every day. I also have been blessed to have good health insurance that has covered a number of expenses that could have financially crushed us. I am further blessed to be in good health and have the ability to generate a good income during these caregiving years. Most importantly, my relationship with God has given me strength, wisdom, encouragement, comfort, patience and the ability to laugh, even when crying seemed like the more natural response. He makes all things possible, and I praise Him for the miracle of transformation he has crafted in me.

One of the lessons I would share with anyone who is or will be a caregiver is this: Please don't try to go it alone. I was overwhelmed as I embarked on my unexpected detour into the caregiving life. I am so incredibly grateful for the loving support of family and friends who brought food, comfort, kind words, hours of assistance and construction support as we converted our home to make it accessible for Sharen. I never would have made it this far without that support.

You are not Superman or Wonder Woman. You have human frailties and limitations. Reach out for help. Talk to family members and friends. Prayer is my number one source of support, which I strongly recommend. Build your own support network. There are countless support groups and a plethora of additional resources to help you in your caregiving journey. I recommend the AARP website as a good starting point: www.aarp.org.

The ultimate blessing in my life has been the joy of sharing it with my amazing wife, Sharen. She is my inspiration every day. She has been God's gift to me. This book is my gift to her—and to you.

Caregiving isn't something we aspire to as we go through life. It usually is thrust upon us. It is never convenient and is filled with challenges. It is also rewarding and transformational in ways that cannot always be adequately expressed. I can honestly say I have received far more than I have given as a caregiver. My cup is overflowing with love and joy. My life is rich beyond belief. And so, if I am ever called upon to be a caregiver again in life?

I would do it in a second!

# ENDNOTES

## Chapter 1

1. Hyrum W. Smith, *What Matters Most: The Power of Living Your Values* (Franklin Covey Co. 2000*)*

2. Adam Fridman, "Living Values Every Day: How Values Influence the Way We Work and Live," www.inc.com, July 17, 2017.

3. Patrick Lencioni.

## Chapter 2

1. Robert K. Greenleaf, *Servant Leadership: A Journey into the Nature of Legitimate Power & Greatness* (Paulist Press 1977).

2. Michael C. Bush, Servant Leaders Create a Great Place to Work for All, from *Servant Leadership in Action*, Edited by Ken Blanchard and Renee Broadwell (Berrett-Kochler Publishers, Inc. 2018).

3. Patrick Lencioni.

## Chapter 3

1. Teresa Amabile and Steven Kramer, *The Progress Principal: Using Small Wins to Ignite Joy, Engagement, and Creativity at Work (*Harvard Business Review Press 2011).

2. Amabile and Kramer. Page 77.

3. Amabile and Kramer. Page 91.

4. *Leadership in Action* Edited by Ken Blanchard and Renee Broadwell (Berrett-Koehler Publishers Inc, 2018)*;* Tom

Mullins *The Leadership Game* (Nashville: Thomas Nelson, 2005).

5. *Leadership in Action,* Mullins. Page 78.
6. *Leadership in Action,* Mullins. Page 78.
7. *Leadership in Action*, Mullins. Page 79.
8. *Leadership in Action*, Mullins. Page 80.
9. *Leadership in Action*, Mullins. Page 80.

## Chapter 4

1. Jon Gordon, *The Power of Positive Leadership* (John Wiley & Sons, Inc. 2017)
2. Gordon. Page 79.
3. Rick Carson, *Taming Your Gremlin* (Harper Collins Publishers, Inc. 2003)
4. Carson. Page 5.
5. Trevor McGlochlin, *3 Ways Positive Leadership Can Make Your Organization More Effective,* (PSI Testing Excellence, August 31, 2018).
6. McGlochlin.
7. Tom Rath, *The Impact of Positive Leadership,* (Gallup, May 13, 2004).
8. Rath.

## Chapter 5

1. Harvard Health Publishing, *In Praise of Gratitude,* (Harvard Medical School, November 2011, updated June 5, 2019).
2. Harvard Health Publishing.
3. John Kralik, *A Simple Act of Gratitude: How Learning to Say Thank You Changed My Life* (Hachette Books 2010). Page 14.
4. Kralik.

5. Gallup and Tom Rath, *StrengthFinder 2.0, Discover your CliftonStrengths* (Gallup Press, CliftonStrengths version 2017).

6. Gallup and Tom Rath.

## Chapter 6

1. Pat Williams, with Jim Denney, *Humility: The Secret Ingredient of Success* (Shiloh Run Press, an imprint of Barbour Publishing, Inc. 2016). Page 37.

2. Ken Blanchard and Phil Hodges, *Lead Like Jesus: LESSONS from the Greatest Leadership Role Model of ALL TIME,* (W Publishing Group, a division of Thomas Nelson, Inc. 2005). Page 67.

3. Patrick Lencioni, *The Ideal Team Player: How to Recognize and Cultivate the Three Essential Virtues,* (Jossey-Boss, A John Wiley & Sons. Inc. Imprint 2016).

4. Lencioni.

5. Lencioni.

6. Scripture taken from the HOLY BIBLE, NEW INTERNATIONAL VERSION, Copyright 1973, 1978, 1984 by International Bible Society. Used by permission of Zondervan. All rights reserved.

7. Kathryn Spink, *Mother Teresa, An Authorized Biography,* (Harper Collins, 2011).

8. Spink.

## Chapter 7

1. Brené Brown, *Dare to Lead: Brave Work. Tough Conversations. Whole Hearts* (Penguin Random House UK 2018). Page 140.

2. Michael Ventura, *Applied Empathy, The New Language of Leadership* (Simon & Shuster, Inc. 2018) Page 99

3. Ventura

4. Travis Bradberry & Jean Greaves, *Emotional Intelligence 2.0* (TalentSmart®, 2009).

## Chapter 8

1. Scripture taken from the HOLY BIBLE, NEW INTERNATIONAL VERSION, Copyright 1973, 1978, 1984 by International Bible Society. Used by permission of Zondervan. All rights reserved.

2. Gary Chapman & Paul White, *The 5 Languages of Appreciation in the Workplace: Empowering Organizations by Encouraging People* (Northfield Publishing, 2011, 2012, 2019). Page 23.

3. Chapman & White. Page 172.

4. From the Chronology in Selected Speeches and Writings/Lincoln by Don E. Fehrenbacher, ed., 1992. Compiled by Lucas Morel.

## Chapter 9

1. Eric Greitens, *Resilience: Hard-Won Wisdom for Living a Better Life* (Mariner Books 2015). Page 23.

2. Sheryl Sandberg & Adam Grant, *Option B: Facing Adversity, Building Resilience, and Finding Joy* (Alfred A. Knopf, New York 2017).

3. Winston Churchill, Churchill Museum, October 29, 1941.

4. Churchill.

## Chapter 10

1. Dale Carnegie Research Institute, *Employee Engagement: It's Time to Go "All-In": Making Engagement a Daily Priority for Leaders* (Dale Carnegie & Associates, Inc. 2018).
2. John C. Maxwell, *The Leader's Greatest Return: Attracting, Developing and Multiplying Leaders* (HarperCollins Leadership, an imprint of Harper Collins Focus LLC 2020). Page 48.
3. Maxwell, Pages 48-49.
4. Jim Clifton & Jim Harter, *It's the Manager: Gallup Finds That The Quality of Managers and Team Leaders Is The Single Biggest Factor In Your Organization's Long-Term Success* (Gallup Press, 2019). Pages 113-116.

## Chapter 11

1. James M. Kouzes & Barry Z. Posner, *A Leader's Legacy* (John Wiley & Sons, Inc., Published by The Leadership Challenge®, A Wiley Brand, 2006). Page 6.
2. Wikipedia.
3. Wikipedia.
4. Wikipedia.
5. Wikipedia.
6. Wikipedia.
7. Kouzes & Posner.

## Chapter 12

1. Wikipedia.
2. Wikipedia.
3. Wikipedia.
4. Jacob Morgan, *The Future Leader: 9 Skills and Mindsets to Succeed in the Next Decade,* (John Wiley & Sons, Inc., 2020).

5. Wikipedia.

6. Marshall Goldsmith, *What Got You Here Won't Get You There,* (Hachette Books, 2007).

## Shocking Statistics About Caregiving

1. AARP, National Alliance for Caregiving, *2020 Report Caregiving in the U.S.,* May 2020.

2. AARP, National Alliance for Caregiving.

3. AARP, National Alliance for Caregiving.

4. AARP, National Alliance for Caregiving.

5. AARP, National Alliance for Caregiving.

6. AARP, *Surprising Out-of-Pocket Costs for Caregivers,* www.aarp.org, October 1, 2019.

7. AARP, National Alliance for Caregiving.

8. AARP, National Alliance for Caregiving.

# ABOUT THE AUTHOR

Ross Woodstock is an executive coach and leadership consultant who helps leaders achieve sustainable growth in their careers. He received coach training from the University of Texas at Dallas and holds a coaching credential from the International Coach Federation. Ross conducts leadership training for high growth leaders in business, government, education and non-profit  organizations. He holds a bachelor's degree in Human Resource Management from Spring Arbor College and a master's degree in Organizational Behavior from University of Texas at Dallas.

For more information about Ross Woodstock, including his speaker's bio, visit www.rosswoodstockingcoaching.com.

Ross and his wife Sharen have two adult children and enjoy life from their deck in East Lansing, Michigan.